# The Current Justification Controversy

# The Current Justification Controversy

O. Palmer Robertson

The Trinity Foundation

*The Current Justification Controversy*


Published by
The Trinity Foundation
Unicoi, Tennessee
http://www. trinityfoundation.org/
ISBN: 0-940931-63-X

# Contents

# About the Author

O. Palmer Robertson received the degrees Doctor of Theology and Master of Theology from Union Theological Seminary in Virginia, in 1966 and 1963; Bachelor of Divinity from Westminster Theological Seminary in 1962; and the Bachelor of Arts from Belhaven College in 1959. He has also engaged in special studies at Cambridge University and the American Institute of Holy Land Studies.

Dr. Robertson was active in the establishment of the Presbyterian Church in America, having given one of the principal messages at the opening assembly. He has worked in various church ministries, in missionary work, as well as in seminary teaching.

He has been Director and Principal of African Bible College, Uganda, since 2002; and Professor of Theology at African Bible College, Malawi, since 1992. He had been Professor of Old Testament at Knox Theological Seminary, Florida, from 1995 to 2002; Adjunct Professor of Old Testament at Knox Theological Seminary from 1992 to 1995; Professor of Old Testament at Covenant Theological Seminary from 1980-1985; Associate Professor of Old Testament Theology at Westminster Theological Seminary from 1971 to 1980; Associate Professor of Biblical Theology at Reformed Theological Seminary from 1967 to 1971.

He has served as pastor of Presbyterian churches in Maryland (Wallace Memorial of Hyattsville), Missouri (Memorial

Presbyterian of St. Louis), Pennsylvania (Immanuel Presbyterian of Malvern), and Mississippi (First Presbyterian of Picayune).

Dr. Robertson is the author of many essays and books. Among his books are *The Christ of the Covenants*, 1980; *Covenants: God's Way with His People*, 1987; *The Books of Nahum, Habakkuk, and Zephaniah* in *The New International Commentary on the Old Testament*, 1990; *Jonah: A Study in Compassion*, 1990; *The Final Word*, 1993; *Psalms in Congregational Celebration*, 1995; *Prophet of the Coming Day of the Lord: The Message of Joel*, 1995; *Understanding the Land of the Bible: A Biblical-Theological Guide*, 1996; *The Israel of God: Yesterday, Today, and Tomorrow*, 2000; *The Genesis of Sex: Sexual Relationships in the First Book of the Bible*, 2002.

Dr. Robertson has been a frequent lecturer and conference speaker at Banner of Truth Conferences, Presbyterian Evangelistic Fellowship Conferences, the PCA Family Conference, Evangelical Theological Society meetings, and the Pensacola Theological Institute. He has lectured in Africa, Europe, Asia, Australia, and Latin America.

# Foreword

THE CURRENT *Justification Controversy* actually refers to an extended dispute on the issue of justification that occurred between 1975 and 1982. Yet a number of factors indicates that the controversy continues even until today.

This summation of the history of the original controversy was first written for publication in *Presbyterion*, the theological journal of Covenant Theological Seminary in St. Louis, Missouri. It was originally approved for publication by the Editorial Committee, but then subsequently was denied publication. The reason given for this reversal was that the material might prove offensive to another respected seminary of the Reformed and Presbyterian family in America.

This decision was appealed to the Eleventh General Assembly of the Presbyterian Church in America, the ecclesiastical body having oversight of the magazine. In its consideration, the argument was made that the Faculty of the Seminary rather than the Assembly should retain the authority to determine what materials were to be published in the journal. This argument prevailed in the Assembly.

In the process of the Assembly's discussion, the article was distributed to approximately one thousand commissioners in attendance. In view of this distribution among this body of ministers and elders, the author did not feel it necessary at that time to seek further publication.

The ongoing character of the original debate twenty years later has led the author to accede to the request for this current publication of the history. Except for minor alterations, the material remains exactly as it was originally presented. It is hoped that an understanding of the history of the controversy may aid the church at large in understanding and evaluating the issue as it continues to manifest itself.

O. Palmer Robertson
April 17, 2003

# The Current Justification Controversy

O. Palmer Robertson

# The Current Justification Controversy

## *Introduction*

BY THE five-hundredth anniversary of Martin Luther's birth in 1483, it might have been expected that the question of the way of a man's justification before God would have been settled, at least in Reformed and evangelical circles. But history demonstrates that such an expectation fails to take account of the resilience inherent in man's natural inclinations to find some role for his own performance in determining his position before God. For the controversy over the relation of works to justification continues to challenge the church.

The recurrence of this issue attests to the correctness of Luther's judgment that justification by faith alone is the doctrine of the standing or falling church. For why else would this single doctrine become the point of dispute throughout the generations?

This historical overview of a current controversy relative to justification is offered in the hope that it may provide a framework by which the church in this day may see more clearly the Gospel issues, and may maintain a fully Biblical perspective. Certainly this brief treatment cannot expect to conclude the matter in the present context. But perhaps it can provide some impetus for advancing the discussion in a way that shall promote the peace and the purity of the church.

Because many of the items reported in this history continue to have contemporary relevance, it seemed appropriate to ask certain individuals involved in the controversy from the beginning to attest to the essential accuracy of the present history insofar as they were able to observe for themselves. The following individuals, representing three different Presbyterian denominations, have offered this testimony. They are: Calvin K. Cummings of the Orthodox Presbyterian Church; W. Stanford Reid of the Presbyterian Church of Canada; and Paul G. Settle of the Presbyterian Church America. Responsibility for any errors remains the author's, who stands ready to make any changes that are shown to be necessary for the sake of historical accuracy.

## 1. *The Beginnings of the Controversy*

The "justification issue" came to the attention of the Faculty of Westminster Theological Seminary in 1975, when certain students were reported to have set forth a position that justification was by faith and by works when being examined by various church bodies. In February 1976, two Faculty members formally addressed the situation, and requested that together with Mr. Norman Shepherd, Associate Professor of Systematic Theology at the Seminary, the Faculty attempt to clarify the matter.

In a previous Faculty discussion of the issue on April 14, 1975, Mr. Shepherd had affirmed that as faith was the instrument of justification, so also works were the instrument of justification. This assertion had drawn a rather vigorous response from various members of the Faculty, since it challenged directly expressions in the doctrinal standards of the Seminary. For the *Westminster Confession of Faith* states that "Faith ... is the alone instrument of justification" (11.2).

Through the early years of the discussion in the Faculty and the Board at the Seminary, it was not clear that Mr. Shepherd actually had taught in the classroom that justification was "by works" as well as "by faith." It was reasoned that a teacher cannot be held responsible for all the ways his students may understand him. It was also proposed that some of Mr. Shepherd's expressions had been exploratory, and were meant only for the Faculty.

However, in the discussions of a special Board-Faculty Committee in 1980, it finally was made clear by tapes of his 1975 lectures that Mr. Shepherd had taught in the classroom that justification was by works as well as by faith. In these lectures, Mr. Shepherd developed extensively the idea that works functioned in a parallel role to faith in justification. He declared that justification presupposes faith; faith is not the ground of justification, but faith is the instrument of justification. In parallel fashion, he declared that justification presupposes good works; good works are not the ground of justification, but good works are the instrument of justification. While faith and works were maintained as distinctive in themselves, each was presented not as the ground but as the instrument of justification.

At this point, certain aspects of the controversy as it originally developed may be noted.

First of all, the problem arose with Mr. Shepherd's affirmation that good works served as the *instrument* or as the *way* of justification. He wished to avoid the idea that good works might serve as the *ground* of justification. But he also plainly stated that good works paralleled faith as the instrument of justification.

Secondly, Mr. Shepherd declared his intention to remain loyal to the teaching of the *Westminster Confession of Faith* and catechisms. This fact must be remembered, and explains much of the divergence in subsequent evaluations of the issue. For in Mr. Shepherd's mind, his teaching was in accord with the standards of the church, although going beyond the *Confession* and catechisms at certain points. The question created by his formulations was whether or not many of his statements actually did accord with the teaching of Scripture and the *Confession.*

Thirdly, Mr. Shepherd defended a "unique" role for faith in justification. Faith was viewed as playing a role in justification that nothing else could fulfill. Indeed, good works also were to be viewed as the instrument or the "way" of justification, but faith was presented as having a distinctive place in justification.

This assertion about faith's "uniqueness" had the effect of allaying the fears of many about Mr. Shepherd's commitment to the Reformed doctrine of justification. But for others, so long as his teaching did not also exclude works as the "way" of justification, the issue remained clouded.

Fourthly, Mr. Shepherd developed from these original formulations a variety of ways by which he might express his distinctive position. Originally he affirmed that good works were the instrument of justification as well as faith. Then for a period of time he proposed that neither faith nor works should be regarded as the "instrument" of justification, since the term "instrument" had the danger of being understood as "instrumental cause." Since only the righteousness of Christ rightly could be understood as the cause of justification, it would be dangerous to speak of either faith or works as the "instrument" of justification. Finally he spoke of faith as "unique" in its role as instrument of justification, while works were the "way" of justification.

Yet through all this divergence of phraseology, a consistency of position was being maintained, indicated by a Faculty Report to the Board dated May 17, 1977. The subsequent evaluations of several outside scholars also noted this consistency. Despite his various modes of expression, faith and good works were presented consistently as parallel to one another in their relation to justification. In this scheme, one could speak of the "unique" role of works as the "way" of justification as well as the "unique" role of faith as the "instrument" of justification. But the distinction between an "instrument" of justification and a "way" of justification in Mr. Shepherd's formulations was difficult to determine.

Fifthly, Mr. Shepherd stressed the organic unity of faith and works in justification. In the end, he could reduce to a single assertion his views about the parallelism of faith and works in justification. He could affirm that justification was "by faith alone" and yet retain his position that justification was by faith and by works. For in his view the "faith" that justifies is itself a work of obedience which is an integral aspect of the larger covenantal response of obedience for justification. If justification is by "obedient faith," it also is by the "obedience of faith." If justification is by a "working faith," it also is by the "works of faith." Even the classic assertion that justification is by "faith alone" thus comes to mean that justification is by faith and by works, since the "faith" that justifies is understood as integral to good works done as the way of justification.

Because of this distinctive perspective, Mr. Shepherd was understood by some to be attacking a recognized enemy by his formulations. He might emphasize that a faith that does not work cannot justify; and so the errors of "easy-believism" would be countered. But because by these expressions he also could mean that the works of faith justify, he was communicating once more the same point that had received such vigorous opposition originally. In a slightly different form he was asserting his view that works as well as faith justify.

Mr. Shepherd cited as Biblical support for his view the statement of James that a man is justified by works as well as by faith (*James* 2:24). In his interpretation, James was speaking of essentially the same justification as Paul, and so could be cited as proof that justification was "by works."

At this point, it may be remembered that both Martin Luther and John Calvin responded rather explicitly to the Roman Catholic analysis of these assertions of James. As Calvin says:

> That we may not then fall into that false reasoning which has deceived the Sophists [the Romanists], we must take notice of the two-fold meaning of the word *justified.* Paul means by it the gratuitous imputation of righteousness before the tribunal of God; and James, the manifestation of righteousness by the conduct, and that before men, as we may gather from the preceding words, "Show me thy faith," etc.*

According to the Reformers, James does not say that "works" must be added to "faith" or included in faith as the way by which men receive God's judicial declaration that their sins are forgiven. In their understanding, James is not even discussing the way to pardon from guilt, as is Paul. To the contrary, James is describing how a man may "show" his faith to

*John Calvin, *Commentaries on the Catholic Epistles*, Eerdmans, 1948, 314f.

be genuine (*James* 2:18), and how faith inevitably will "come to fulness" or "fruition" in good works (*James* 2:22).

Subsequent discussion of the "justification" issue must begin with a full awareness of the original state of the matter. Otherwise, later assertions by Mr. Shepherd that actually continue his initial perspective will be heard only as affirmations of traditional orthodoxy. The controversy began with Mr. Shepherd's assertion that works paralleled faith as the *instrument* of justification. The issue continued as Mr. Shepherd insisted that works were the *way* of justification, and that faith included in its essence the good works that justify.

## *2. The October 1976 Paper*

The Faculty of Westminster Seminary could not easily resolve the issues raised by Mr. Shepherd's distinctive formulations on the doctrine of justification. He continued to affirm all the classic modes of expression, although having some hesitation about saying that justification was by faith alone.

But he also said other things. If justification was "by faith," it also was "by works."

So in May 1976, the Faculty requested Mr. Shepherd to prepare a paper explaining his own view on the statement of the Westminster Standards that faith is the alone instrument of justification. His paper was to serve as the basis for a Faculty discussion later in the year.

Consequently, a paper by Mr. Shepherd titled "The Relation of Good Works to Justification in the Westminster Standards" became the basis for a Faculty discussion on October 1 and 2, 1976.

This paper is fifty-three pages in length. It represents the fullest exposition of Mr. Shepherd's views to date. It is crucial to all the discussion that has arisen since its presentation to the Faculty.

The paper originally was to be restricted to a Faculty discussion to be held on October 1 and 2, 1976. This intent is stated explicitly on its cover. But with the author's full participation and consent, the paper became the object of intensive deliberation within the Faculty for the next eighteen months. The Board and administration of the Seminary were included, as were visiting Faculty.

If Mr. Shepherd had withdrawn his paper after the first meeting, and had renounced the disputed points he had proposed in the paper, then the role of the document would be something other than it is today. But he chose to defend the various propositions of the paper for a period of over eighteen months in a context of very intensive discussion with Board and Faculty. He himself determined that the paper function in this manner by defending its contents paragraph by paragraph over this lengthy period. Mr. Shepherd's October 1976 paper therefore has become crucial to understanding the issues under consideration.

In November 1978, the Board of Trustees made this document along with the other papers of the discussion available to the public. By this action, the Board offered its evaluation of the continuing significance of the paper in understanding Mr. Shepherd's position.

But what was the content of the paper? What were the main points that Mr. Shepherd made?

First, Mr. Shepherd affirmed that not only faith, but also the concrete actions of repentance are necessary as the way of justification (13-15).

In making this affirmation, appeal was made to the statement of the *Westminster Confession of Faith*, that repentance was so essential to salvation that "none may expect pardon without it" (*WCF* 15.3). Elsewhere the *Westminster Confession* affirms that "all other saving graces" will ever accompany the faith that justifies (*WCF* 11.2).

While placing his analysis in the framework of classic Confessional statements, Mr. Shepherd's formulations were certain to engender controversy. For although it is commonly acknowledged that the grace of repentance in terms of a wholehearted commitment to turn from sin always will accompany the faith that justifies, it is somewhat different to say that specific actions arising from repentance also are necessary to be carried out as the way of justification. For to say that concrete actions of repentance are necessary as the way of justification is to join works to faith as the way of justification.

Secondly, Mr. Shepherd affirmed that not only faith and actions of repentance are necessary as the way of justification. Also works that take time, including even the diligent use of the outward means of grace, are necessary for justification (15, 17).

In a subsequent paper, Mr. Shepherd attempted to explain his statement that the diligent use of the means of grace was necessary for justification. He indicated that he intended to refer to the justification of the last day (March 1, 1978 paper, 4f.).

Yet this explanation hardly could prove adequate to relieve the tension felt by many between Mr. Shepherd's statements and the assertions of Scripture. For little if any evidence may be found in Scripture that *forgiveness* of sins shall occur in the judgment of the last day. Essential to "justification" is the forgiveness of sins, yet the unbeliever certainly will not be forgiven at the last day. The believer already stands justified. The cleansing forgiveness associated with sanctification hardly will be needed by the saints who already will have been changed into the glorious likeness of Christ at his appearing.

Indeed, a "vindication" of the status of the believer shall occur at the last judgment. He shall be "openly acknowledged, and acquitted in the day of judgment" (*Shorter Catechism* Q. 38). But in that vindication, good works arising from repentance shall function only as fruit and evidence of the unshakable status of justification which had been realized at the moment of believing.

Mr. Shepherd's efforts to explain his statement about the necessity of good works as the way of justification could not relieve the tension created by his earlier assertions. Good works indeed may be perceived as the necessary fruit and evidence of the faith that justifies, but good works cannot be acknowledged as the way of justification without creating confusion.

A third point made by Mr. Shepherd in his October 1976 paper ultimately proved to be significant in clarifying his whole system of thought about the relation of good works to justification. In the October paper, Mr. Shepherd posits that good works are necessary to maintain a person in the state of justification (14). In order to continue in justification, a person must perform good works.

In various subsequent discussions, Mr. Shepherd affirmed that a person could lose his justification. He proposed that an individual who was elect according to the election of *Ephesians* 1 could become non-elect if he did not continue to walk in covenant faithfulness.*

* See the discussion of the "Downingtown Conference" in chapter 5 below.

So when Mr. Shepherd posited the necessity of good works for justification in the last judgment, and the necessity of the diligent use of the means of grace for continuing in justification, he was affirming that the justified actually could become non-justified. In this construction, good works must be seen as actually necessary to maintain a person in a state of justification.

Mr. Shepherd later presented as his model for this argumentation the exile of Israel under the old covenant. He also found support in the illustration of the branches cut off from Christ in the new covenant. For from his perspective these cut-off branches first were savingly united to Christ.*

According to Mr. Shepherd, the election of individuals described in *Ephesians* 1 consisted of the same kind of election experienced by Israel as a nation. Israel's movement to a state of non-election thus could serve as a warning to the elect of the new covenant that they too could become non-elect.†

As the full consequences of Mr. Shepherd's teaching became apparent, the controversy over his formulations inevitably deepened. For if the only election and justification that the sinner who trusts in Christ can know may be lost, then all enduring assurance is lost. It was this point in particular that served ultimately to clarify the implications of Mr. Shepherd's various formulations, and to evoke a steady resistance to his teachings. For he clearly had introduced a new element into

* See his article on "The Covenant Context for Evangelism" in *The New Testament Student and Theology*, Presbyterian and Reformed (1976), Vol. III, 64f.

† "Reprobation in Covenant Perspective: The Biblical Doctrine," a lecture given by Mr. Shepherd to the Christian Reformed Minister's Institute, Grand Rapids, Michigan, June 1978.

the classic formulations of the Reformers when he declared that justification and election by God could be lost.

Fourthly, Mr. Shepherd modified the generally accepted understanding of the proper pattern of the Gospel call for justification. In his view, "the command to believe, the command to repent and be baptized, and the command to follow Christ doing as he commanded are not ultimately different answers" to the question concerning how a man is to be justified. For although Paul told the Philippian jailer that he must believe to be saved, he just as well could have told him to rise up and follow Christ. For "to ask for obedience is not a fundamentally different thing than to ask for faith, though faith and obedience may be distinguished as descriptive of a single total response from different perspectives" (October 1976 paper, 51).

In analyzing these assertions, it must be remembered that the subject under discussion was the way to *justification.* "Salvation" in the broader sense includes sanctification as well as justification, and clearly obedience performed by faith is an essential aspect of holiness.

But Mr. Shepherd by his formulations had merged faith and obedience as a "single total response" which brings justification. According to his view, faith is united with works as a single response to the Gospel call for justification. As a consequence, justification is by faith and by works, or by faith/works, or by the works of faith. Or, justification is by "obedient faith," which could be interchanged with "faithful obedience."

In his October 1976 paper, Mr. Shepherd developed a distinctive viewpoint on the relation of works to justification. The distinctive expressions of this paper he defended vigorously for over eighteen months, through numerous daylong discussions with Board and Faculty.

It is for this reason that the October 1976 paper continues to be crucial in analyzing later statements of Mr. Shepherd. Rather than proving to be "experimental" and "incidental" to the thought-patterns of Mr. Shepherd, these formulations he defended as firm convictions.

The justification controversy had arisen out of Mr. Shepherd's assertions that justification was "by works" as well as "by faith." The October 1976 paper uncovered more fully the framework from which this perspective arose.

## *3. Reactions to the October 1976 Paper (October 1976 – February 1979)*

Mr. Shepherd's October 1976 paper required some response. The distinctive proposals of the paper were: (1) that concrete actions of repentance were the way of justification; (2) that works of faith that take time were necessary for justification; (3) that the diligent use of the outward means of grace maintained justification; and (4) that in the call of the Gospel for justification, the sinner might just as well be told to follow Christ as to believe in Christ, since faith and obedience were a single unified response of the sinner for justification.

The Faculty conducted intensive discussions on this paper for a period of eighteen months. Their questions often related to the effort to determine whether actual error was being taught in Mr. Shepherd's formulations, or whether Mr. Shepherd's modes of expression simply were misleading because of their lack of clarity. The Faculty restricted itself specifically to the issue of justification, although it was known by some that his views on related issues such as the nature of the covenant and the sacrament of baptism also would be controversial.

After several months of discussion, the Faculty majority noted that Mr. Shepherd "continues to defend his views and expressions" as found in the October 1976 and April 1977 papers. While acknowledging some clarifications, they concluded "that certain of Mr. Shepherd's statements on the subject of justification require further consideration and modification to avoid obscuring the teaching of the Scriptures and the Westminster Standards" (Faculty Minutes of May 3, 1977, meeting). While two members of the Faculty recorded their negative votes because they favored an even stronger statement, this adopted motion indicates the judgment of the Faculty after several months of intensive discussion. Mr. Shepherd had continued to defend his original "views and expressions," and modification was necessary to avoid obscuring the Biblical teaching on justification despite some clarification.

But in April 1978, a majority of the Faculty concluded that although Mr. Shepherd's "structure of argumentation seems bound to create misunderstanding," his formulations fell within the toleration limits of the Westminster Standards (April 25, 1978, Report to the Board). The Faculty urged Mr. Shepherd to use different means of argument "less open to misunderstanding" to explain his legitimate concerns.

The implications of this conclusion are rather striking. Mr. Shepherd's formulations on the central doctrine of justification almost certainly will mislead the church into thinking that somehow works were the way of justification. Yet these formulations were not out of accord with the *Westminster Confession.*

The tension involved in this conclusion found explicit expression in a statement which President Edmund P. Clowney read to the Faculty on the day the Faculty made its April 1978 decision. In his statement, Dr. Clowney observed that in Mr. Shepherd's argument, good works are "included in repentance and joined to faith as a requirement for justification" (3). Dr. Clowney analyzed Mr. Shepherd's viewpoint as representing a "sharp break with the Princeton theology of Charles Hodge" because he had inserted "new obedience along with repentance and faith before justification" (2). He concluded that "when [Mr. Shepherd] insists on moving obedience back from the way to the entering of the way it is plain that his formulation differs significantly from the catechism" (5).

Yet in the end, Dr. Clowney proceeded to urge that the Faculty not find the theology of Mr. Shepherd out of accord with the "system of doctrine" found in the Westminster Standards.

A vigorous dissent from this Report as adopted by the majority of the Faculty was registered by Philip E. Hughes, Visiting Professor of New Testament at the Seminary. Dr. Hughes expressed amazement that he would find himself having to register a protest against a decision of the Faculty of Westminster Seminary regarding the expression of their views on the doctrine of justification. He concentrated specifically on the proposal that faith cannot be isolated from works in justification. He insisted that as a matter of fact faith *must* be isolated from its works in justification.

Dr. Richard B. Gaffin, Jr., of the Faculty of Westminster responded to these expressions of Dr. Hughes. He argued that the reference to "holiness without which no one shall see the Lord" (*Hebrews* 12:14) indicated that sanctification *must* accompany justification. He declared that Paul's exclusion of "works of the law" from justification must not be understood as minimizing the necessary role of "good works" in the life of every believer. He underscored the fundamental role of the life-transformation effected by union with Christ as a crucial factor in appreciating the vital link between justification and sanctification.

Yet it does not appear that Dr. Gaffin was affirming precisely the same thing as that which was found in the formulations of Mr. Shepherd. Although he might defend the statement that good works are necessary for "continuing" in a state of justification, he never implied as did Mr. Shepherd that the justified could become unjustified, or that the elect according to *Ephesians* 1 could become reprobate. He did not express agreement with Mr. Shepherd's conclusion based on his comparison between James and Paul that the justification about which Paul speaks is "by works." He did not affirm that good works that take time are the "way" of justification.

Although Dr. Gaffin defended Mr. Shepherd, it is not clear that this defense was in support of those aspects of Mr. Shepherd's formulations that constituted his distinctive approach. Instead, Dr. Gaffin seems to have been supporting the customary Reformed formulation that faith alone justifies, although the faith that justifies is never alone.

The Board of Westminster in May 1978 declined to concur with the judgment of the Faculty majority in its support of Mr. Shepherd. Instead, it "received" the Report of the Faculty, and granted Mr. Shepherd a leave of absence so he could study the matter further. In a subsequent meeting, the Board authorized its members to share with the public the various documents of the discussion, including the October 1976 paper (Board action of November 14, 1978).

Prior to these actions, the Board had been involved in repeated discussion of the October 1976 paper. The only written response by a Board member came in the form of a brief but pointed critique offered by Dr. W. Stanford Reid. Dr. Reid noted that Mr. Shepherd apparently was laying a "foundation for a doctrine of works-righteousness which is in direct contradiction to the Scriptures."

The Board had further registered its concern over the October 1976 paper by asking Mr. Shepherd to reformulate four statements in particular. These statements the Board regarded as significantly misleading or erroneous.

Mr. Shepherd had offered his reformulations at a subsequent meeting of the Board, and their substance became a part of the discussion. The Faculty Report to the Board later indicated that in its judgment these reformulations were "alterations in wording rather than in the substance of Mr. Shepherd's position" (Faculty Report of April 25, 1978).

On February 8, 1979, the President presented a new proposal to the Board. He recommended that the Board find "no sufficient cause" to continue the discussion of Mr. Shepherd's views. In contrast with his previous evaluations, the President now stated that "Mr. Shepherd's views as they have been presented to the Board do not call into question his adherence to the *Westminster Confession of Faith*.... [h]e does not question or challenge the Reformed doctrine of justification by faith alone" (Board Minutes of February 9, 1979, 16-17). This statement proceeded to note that Mr. Shepherd had clarified some of his statements, and had recognized that some of his earlier formulations were obscure, misleading, or ambiguous. Mr. Shepherd was urged to use wisdom in communicating Biblical doctrine.

At this meeting, Mr. Shepherd introduced to the Board his paper titled *The Grace of Justification.* His paper on *Thirty-four Theses on Justification in Relation to Faith, Repentance, and Good Works*, which currently was being evaluated by the Presbytery of Philadelphia of the Orthodox Presbyterian Church, also was included as a basis for discussion.

After a lengthy period of interaction, the recommendation of the President passed by a vote of eleven to eight. Five Board members recorded their negative votes.

So in February 1979 the long struggle over the question of Mr. Shepherd's formulations about the distinctive role of works in justification was ended – or so it seemed. Although regretting the misunderstanding that had been created by his distinct expressions, Mr. Shepherd had held essentially to the substance of his formulations as developed in the October 1976 paper, as indicated by the Faculty Report. The modification of certain phrases as requested by the Board had not changed the substance of his position. Good works were necessary as the way of justification, and not simply as its fruit. Walking in the way of obedience was necessary to maintain justification. The sinner seeking justification might just as well be told to follow Jesus as to believe in Jesus.

Mr. Shepherd was commended for his fresh insights into these questions. He also was urged to be more careful in the manner in which he formulated his views. He was told by the Faculty that his structure of argumentation seemed bound to create misunderstanding on the doctrine of justification.

But by this action, he had been exonerated by the Board. His teaching had been judged to fall within the limits tolerated by Scripture and the *Confession*. The case appeared to be closed by an eleven to eight vote of the Board of Trustees.

## 4. The Issue before the Presbytery (1977-1981)

Charges were filed formally against Mr. Shepherd in Philadelphia Presbytery of the Orthodox Presbyterian Church on May 27, 1977, and presented to the meeting of Presbytery held on September 30, 1977. This point needs to be emphasized, since those critical of Mr. Shepherd's views have been accused of failing to follow proper judicial procedure.

It ought to be recognized that filing formal charges is not the only Scriptural method for carrying out a theological dispute. In fact, ecclesiastical litigation of one brother against another often may prove to be a most unhealthy procedure in resolving theological differences.

Yet in all fairness, it ought to be noted by those critical of the opponents of Mr. Shepherd's views that charges were filed. Amidst a most solemn and formal reading of warnings against anyone who dared to present accusations against a brother, charges were filed.

These charges were founded on the material that had been the basis of discussion in the Faculty of Westminster Seminary for the previous months. Some ground could have been found in the testimonies of students who had been taught by Mr. Shepherd, but any such testimony obviously could be disputed.

Not until three years later were tapes of Mr. Shepherd's 1975 class lectures made available. At that time it became evident that he explicitly had been teaching in the classroom that justification was "by works" as well as "by faith."

So the charges rested on the material that had been made available to the Faculty and Board of the Seminary. The fifty-three page paper of October 1976 by Mr. Shepherd on the relation of good works to justification served as a partial ground on which the charges in Presbytery were founded.

Now the response to this action became very intense. A letter from the President of Westminster Seminary, Edmund Clowney, urged the Presbytery not to admit these charges, since they were founded on materials private to the Board and Faculty of Westminster Seminary. A letter from the Faculty to the Presbytery followed shortly, arguing along the same line. Mr. Shepherd also indicated that he did not desire to be judged by the October 1976 paper.

After much deliberation, and in response to the recommendation of a special committee, the Presbytery acceded to the request made by the President and Faculty of Westminster Seminary. The October 1976 paper and all other testimony arising from it were not to be admitted as evidence in the Presbytery. For, it was argued, the rights of academic freedom must be protected. A professor must be allowed to explore fresh modes of expression without fear of reprisal. How can theological inquiry expect to progress apart from a carefully guarded freedom to explore and to experiment in an honest effort to capture more Biblical modes of expression?

So the decision of Presbytery may be defended. A court of Christ's church must provide its members liberty to probe more deeply into the truth of God's Word.

But at the same time, the implications of the decision of Presbytery must be considered with care. For, in effect, the Presbytery relinquished its right of supervision over one of its own ministers. In effect, the academic community of the Seminary was judged by Presbytery to possess a right of supervision over its ministers that was above its own.

By refusing to look at the documents themselves, the Presbytery allowed a majority of the Seminary Faculty to determine when the theological expressions of a minister were to be regarded as "experimental" and "academic," without reviewing the substance of the question itself.

Central to the discussion within the Seminary had been the question of whether or not Mr. Shepherd's later formulations represented adequate modifications or retractions of the erroneous or misleading statements that he had defended so constantly. The Presbytery allowed a majority of the Seminary Board and Faculty to decide, without subject to review, that the expressions continuing to be maintained by Mr. Shepherd and defended by him already for a full year should be discarded as a basis for ecclesiastical trial or investigation.

Even during the time in which the Presbytery was determining whether or not to admit the October 1976 paper, that document was continuing to provide the basis for discussion within the Seminary community. Just a few days before charges were filed with the Presbytery, the Faculty had reported to the Board that "certain of Mr. Shepherd's statements on the subject of justification require further consideration and modification to avoid obscuring the teaching of Scripture and of the Westminster Standards" (May 17, 1977 Report). This Report cited four statements from the October 1976 paper as illustrative of the problems associated with Mr. Shepherd's mode of expression.

Several months after the charges had been presented to the Presbytery, in March 1978, Mr. Shepherd submitted to the Board a revised form of these same four statements from the October 1976 paper. So it is quite clear that although acknowledged to be a "study paper," Mr. Shepherd's October 1976 paper continued to serve as the basis of Board-Faculty discussions of the issue even during the time that the Presbytery was determining whether or not to admit the paper as evidence in the charges that had been presented.

The decision of the Presbytery not to admit the October 1976 paper as evidence was appealed to the General Assembly of the Orthodox Presbyterian Church. The appeal was denied.

When the Board of the Seminary decided in November 1978 to release to the public all the papers related to the justification discussion, including the October 1976 paper, the situation changed materially. Now the October 1976 paper fell into the realm of public domain, and conceivably could have become a basis for newly issued judicial charges.

Mr. Shepherd at that point submitted to the Presbytery his *Thirty-four Theses on Justification in Relation to Faith, Repentance, and Good Works.* As an alternative to pursuing charges further in the Presbytery, the *Thirty-four Theses* were offered as doctrinal formulations seriously and reasonably proposed which the church might evaluate (see the OPC *Form of Government*, XII, 1). This possibility had been discussed with those who previously had been involved in filing charges, and the procedure generally had been agreeable to them.

So the Presbytery committed itself to the task of debating for a full year these brief statements on justification offered by Mr. Shepherd. Among the formulations most contested were the following:

> The Pauline affirmation in *Romans* 2:13, "The doers of the Law will be justified," is . . . to be understood . . . in the sense that faithful disciples of the Lord Jesus Christ will be justified (Thesis 20).
>
> The exclusive ground of the justification of the be-

> liever in the state of justification is the righteousness of Jesus Christ, but his obedience ... is necessary to his continuing in a state of justification (Thesis 21).
>
> The righteousness of Jesus Christ ever remains the exclusive ground of the believer's justification, but the personal godliness of the believer is also necessary for his justification in the judgment of the last day (*Matthew* 7:21-33; 25:31-46; *Hebrews* 12:14) (Thesis 22).
>
> [G]ood works ... though not the ground of [the believer's] justification, are nevertheless necessary for justification (Thesis 23).

In the process of its discussion as a "committee of the whole," the Presbytery approved most of the *Thirty-four Theses.* When the court finally reconstituted itself in January 1980, the motion was made that the report of the "committee of the whole" to the effect that the *Thirty-four Theses* be found in accord with Scripture and the *Confession* be adopted. The motion failed by a tie vote. A motion then was made to find the *Thirty-four Theses* out of accord with Scripture and the *Confession.* This motion also failed by a larger majority.

A Complaint was filed against the Presbytery's failure to sustain the report of the committee of the whole. This complaint was denied by a substantial majority in a later meeting of Presbytery.

After a year's deliberation, the Presbytery was evenly divided. It could not decide whether these formulations were in accord with Scripture and the *Confession.* In effect, the prediction of the Faculty that Mr. Shepherd's "structure of argumentation seems bound to create misunderstanding" proved to be accurate.

Mr. Shepherd had offered an apology for his earlier October 1976 paper when he presented the *Thirty-four Theses* in 1978 to the Presbytery. He had acknowledged that the formulations of the October paper were at points obscure or misleading and at other points loosely written or ambiguous.

But a careful comparison of the *These*s with the October paper makes it fairly apparent that all the distinctive expressions of the October paper find their condensed counterpart in the *Thirty-four Theses.* Mr. Shepherd did not alter his position in the *Thirty-four Theses*, although his distinctive position was more immediately apparent in the October 1976 paper because of its fuller development of his views.

But now what was the Presbytery to do? They had approved Mr. Shepherd's call as one responsible for training men for the Christian ministry, and yet they could not endorse his distinctive formulations on the central doctrine of justification as being in accord with Scripture and the *Confession.*

The Presbytery established a committee to study the matter, and to return with recommendations. The committee subsequently recommended that the Presbytery pursue the matter no further unless formal charges were brought against Mr. Shepherd.

This decision was appealed to the 1981 General Assembly of the Orthodox Presbyterian Church. The argument was made that the Presbytery originally had refused to receive charges; that the Presbytery had then adopted the route of deliberating the *Thirty-four Theses*; and that having chosen this route, it was the Presbytery's responsibility to resolve the matter either by continuing its discussion or by drawing up charges itself that the matter might be adjudicated properly.

The appeal was denied. Individuals who continued to have concerns were told they could initiate judicial proceedings.

The decision of the Assembly placed the burden of responsibility on concerned individuals within the Presbytery.

In any case, a very ambiguous situation prevailed. Mr. Shepherd's distinctive formulations had neither been condemned nor approved by his Presbytery. As a consequence, a man whose formulations on the crucial doctrine of justification had failed to find the approval of his own Presbytery continued to prepare men for the Gospel ministry.

## 5. *The Downingtown Conference (Fall 1978)*

Some uniformity of perspective had to be achieved in the Seminary community once a majority vote of the Faculty supportive of Mr. Shepherd had been registered, particularly since in May 1978 the Board had only "received" the Report of the Faculty. Because the matter under discussion was understood by some as touching the heart of the Gospel rather than a peripheral issue, it is understandable that achieving a mere majority vote in a single Faculty meeting could not be expected to end the matter altogether.

The situation was further complicated by the tension inherent in the decision that had been made by the Faculty in April 1978. During the discussion which led to the adoption of the Faculty Report, the President had read a statement in which he affirmed that "when [Mr. Shepherd] insists on moving obedience back from the way to the entering of the way it is plain that his formulation differs significantly from the catechism" (5). Although the adopted Report found Mr. Shepherd's theology to fall within the tolerance limits of the *Confession*, it also stated that his very "structure of argumentation seems bound to create misunderstanding" (April 25, 1978 Report). These inherent tensions in the decision of the Faculty almost guaranteed that the issue could not be laid to rest by a simple majority vote.

So the President determined to invite certain principal participants in the discussion to join in a special conference late in 1978. Arrangements were made at the Downingtown Inn, located in a community west of Philadelphia. Those who were to participate in the conference included President Edmund P. Clowney, Dean Robert G. Strimple, Norman Shepherd, W. Robert Godfrey, Richard B. Gaffin, Jr., Meredith G. Kline (visiting professor from Gordon-Conwell Seminary), and O. Palmer Robertson. Upon being invited, Mr. Robertson indicated that he would be happy to participate, but that he felt progress could be made only through fresh insights offered by the inclusion of individuals from the broader church community. He requested that noteworthy theologians from his denomination be invited to participate in the conference.

President Clowney denied this request. In light of this denial, Mr. Robertson declined the invitation to participate in the conference. Professor Leslie W. Sloat was then invited to join the group.

At the beginning of the consultation, it was determined that discussion primarily would be restricted to the *Thirty-four Theses* of Mr. Shepherd. The Faculty as a whole had not discussed the *Theses*, and they currently were before the Presbytery.

Mr. Kline objected to this limitation, indicating that he felt the broader framework of Mr. Shepherd's theological thinking needed to be discussed as the basis for analyzing the ultimate intent of some of the more ambiguous *Theses*. But President Clowney urged that the group limit itself to an analysis of the *Thirty-four Theses*.

After several hours of discussion, a general sense of progress in understanding seemed to prevail. But the discussion then took a sudden turn. In response to a remark from Mr. Godfrey, Mr. Shepherd affirmed that he believed it was possible for a person to lose his justification.

The introduction of this rather startling assertion into the discussion had the effect of shattering whatever accord had been reached. The significance of the particular "covenant perspective" of Mr. Shepherd that had been a concern originally to Mr. Kline finally had surfaced. But time and agenda did not allow for a satisfactory investigation into this all-embracing question.

As a consequence, the Downingtown Conference failed to achieve its goal. Uniformity of perspective could not be reached.

Yet the Conference did serve to underscore certain points about the issues under discussion. Some of Mr. Shepherd's *Thirty-four Theses* were of such a nature that by slight modification or clarification they could be read so that they accorded with Scripture and the *Confession*. Yet when they were placed in the larger framework of his distinctive covenantal approach, problems of a serious nature emerged.

One illustration may be seen in Mr. Shepherd's twenty-first *Thesis*, which reads:

> The exclusive ground of the justification of the believer in the state of justification is the righteousness of Jesus Christ, but his obedience, which is simply the perseverance of the saints in the way of truth and righteousness, is necessary to his continuing in a state of justification (*Hebrews* 3:6,14).

This statement, by slight modification or clarification, could be read in a way that would protect the balance found in the expressions of Scripture or the Westminster Standards. Obedience must flow from faith, and the faith that does not produce obedience is no-faith. In this sense, obedience has a "necessary" relation to justification.

Yet the phraseology of the *Thesis* itself is misleading. As it stands, the words affirm that obedience is "necessary" for "continuing" in a state of justification, implying the possibility that justification may be lost. When this *Thesis* is read in the framework of Mr. Shepherd's affirmation at Downingtown that a person can lose his justification, a serious problem emerges. Mr. Shepherd communicates by this *Thesis* the idea that a person actually may pass from a justified to a non-justified status. Having been justified in accord with the justification described in *Romans* 3-5, a person actually may become unjustified if he does not continue to perform good works.

So the participants of the Downingtown Conference looked very briefly into Mr. Shepherd's distinctive covenantal perspective. What they saw certainly could not contribute to a process of unifying the Faculty and the Seminary.

### *6. The "Committee to Draw Up a Statement" (May 1979 – May 1980)*

The Board of Trustees had not adopted the April 1978 majority Report of the Faculty supportive of Mr. Shepherd. But in February 1979 the Board of Trustees voted eleven to eight to support the recommendation of President Clowney that it find "no sufficient cause to pursue further its inquiries into the teaching of Professor Norman Shepherd regarding the doctrine of justification by faith." This closely divided vote could not display a uniformity of perspective. As a matter of fact, the strong conviction of dissenting Board members is seen in the fact that five members registered their negative votes on the motion.

Further evidence that the issue was not yet satisfactorily resolved appeared almost immediately. By the next Board meeting, in May 1979, ten members had signed a statement declaring that in their judgment the Board had acted prematurely and unsuitably in concluding the matter. The Petition noted that the matter had not yet been resolved in the Presbytery, and that it had "not been demonstrated that [Mr. Shepherd's] formulations on justification" were "in conformity with Scripture and the standards of the Seminary." Signers of this Petition to the Board were Everett Bean, Calvin K. Cummings, Donald C. Graham, Terry L. Gyger, Norman C. Hoeflinger, Charles W. Krahe, Jr., W. Stanford Reid, Kenneth L. Ryskamp, Paul G. Settle, and Murray Forst Thompson (emeritus member).

In response to this Petition, President Clowney proposed to the Board in May 1979 that the Seminary community commit itself to work harder toward a genuine reconciliation. He stated that in fairness to Mr. Shepherd, the Board could not reopen its examination of his views apart from a formal charge. Yet the appeal of the Petitioners for a clarification of the Seminary's position could be heard.

So he recommended that a special Board-Faculty Committee be given the responsibility of preparing a study paper and statement on the doctrine of justification by faith. Membership of this Committee of five would be divided between individuals representing the diverging positions on the issue.

*The Committee's Task*

Several aspects of this motion as presented to the Board need to be noted. First of all, the proposal clearly recognized that the issue by no means was over. The very constituency of the Committee indicates the depth of the rift still existent in Board and Faculty.

At the same time, the President's proposal worked with the assumption that the ten Petitioners to the Board would be satisfied with an effort to write a statement reconciling them to the decision that Mr. Shepherd's position would continue to be acceptable to the Seminary. As the only alternative to this proposal, the President called for formal charges against Mr. Shepherd, showing that his teaching violated the doctrinal standard of the Seminary. In so doing, the President passed by the several other options for dealing with the issue that ultimately became the procedure of the Board.

Only after a significant amendment had been introduced as a modification of the original form of the motion was the President's proposal adopted by the Board. This amendment stated that the Committee was to "seek the counsel...of other theological scholars in discharging its task."

The effect of this amendment is crucial for understanding the precise task being assigned this special Committee. Did the amended form of the motion accent the conclusion of the President that a reopening of the issue respecting Mr. Shepherd's formulations could not be accomplished in fairness to Mr. Shepherd in any way other than the issuing of a formal charge that his teaching violated the doctrinal standard of the Seminary? Or did the amended form of the motion offer another alternative? Did it intend that the Committee ask a select group of theologians outside the immediate community of the Seminary to confer with this Committee in writing a "statement and study paper," thereby involving these "outside theologians" in some form of evaluation of Mr. Shepherd's formulations?

Taken in itself, the amended motion as passed in the Board possesses sufficient ambiguity so that its commission could be interpreted in either of these two ways. The President consistently insisted that the amended motion had to be understood in the light of his introductory remarks in his report to the Board. The issue had not been reopened, and the task of the Committee was to compose a statement which could be issued to the public, reassuring them of the continuing orthodoxy of Westminster Seminary.

But several factors indicate that the amendment had the effect of altering significantly the task assigned to the Committee. These "outside theologians" somehow would have to evaluate Mr. Shepherd's theological statements if they were to contribute meaningfully to the writing of a statement on justification in the current context. For why otherwise should a Committee of Westminster Theological Seminary's Board and Faculty need to consult with "outside theologians" regarding a statement on the central doctrine of justification? Were they not capable of working out such a statement?

"Outside theologians" had to be included because the Seminary's Board and Faculty were deadlocked on the issue. They could be of no real help if they were denied access to the total framework of the discussion. Only then could they be expected to offer independent evaluation of the issues at hand. While the President's original motion clearly did not envision such a broadening of the issue, the force of the amendment to include "outside theologians" by the very nature of the case intended to do precisely what the President did not desire at this point.

The immediate response of the Faculty and the newly constituted Committee confirms this analysis. At the next meeting of the Faculty, a motion was made that this new Committee be directed not to share Mr. Shepherd's October 1976 paper with the "outside theologians" being consulted. This motion was defeated, and so the Committee indirectly was given the go-ahead in sharing this crucial document with the "outside theologians."

But why should such a motion be made if it was not generally understood by the Faculty that the "outside theologians" would be asked to evaluate Mr. Shepherd's theology? Although this motion to exclude the October 1976 paper was supported by the President, its defeat underscores the Faculty's assessment of the task of this Committee as being one that involved a re-opening of the issue of Mr. Shepherd's views.

Further indicators that the Committee originally understood its task as involving some form of reassessment of Mr. Shepherd's views may be seen in the early actions of the Committee itself. In the first telephone conference of the Committee, it was agreed that all the documents related to the justification issue would be made available to the "outside theologians," including specifically Mr. Shepherd's October 1976 paper.

In an early communication as a member of the Committee, Board member Thomas Vanden Heuvel expressed his opinion that "all the relevant documents" ought to be shared, and that the "outside theologians" should have access to "the entire file." The form of advice being sought was "the opinion on the part of each of the experts regarding the legitimacy of the views of Norman Shepherd in the light of Scripture and the *Westminster Confession*" (letter to the Committee dated September 12, 1979).

After a period of study, this Committee indicated that in its preliminary judgment, the Board had acted prematurely in concluding its investigation of Mr. Shepherd's views. This first Report of the Committee clearly indicates that in its earlier stages the Committee assumed that a reassessment of Mr. Shepherd's views was a part of its task.

So it seems fairly clear that the Committee to Draw Up a Statement originally understood its task to include some reevaluation of Mr. Shepherd's formulations. The amendment to the President's original motion which required a consultation with "outside theologians" changed the direction of the proposal of the President. Now the Committee had the responsibility of writing a "statement and study paper" in consultation with outside theologians which would interact directly with the serious issue which continued to divide Board and Faculty.

*The Committee's Procedures*

Those elected by the Board to this special Committee were Rev. Thomas Vanden Heuvel as one who had previously supported the Board's action to see no cause for pursuing further the "justification issue"; Rev. Paul G. Settle as one who had signed the Petition which stated that the Board had acted prematurely in concluding the issue; and Mr. Kenneth Ryskamp, Esquire, viewed as one who had been generally "neutral" with respect to Mr. Shepherd, although he had been among the ten Board members who had signed the recent Petition which reopened the issue.

Those elected by the Faculty to this Committee were Dr. Richard B. Gaffin, Jr., viewed as one who defended Mr. Shepherd's expressions; and Dr. O. Palmer Robertson, viewed as one who had been critical of Mr. Shepherd's expressions.

Non-voting members of the Committee were the Chairman of the Board, Mr. Theodore Pappas; and the President of the Seminary, Dr. Edmund P. Clowney. Mr. Pappas, for a variety of reasons, was not able to participate in the meetings of the Committee. Mr. Ryskamp served as chairman.

The Committee began its meetings with a series of telephone conferences. Various noteworthy theologians outside the Seminary community who might be consulted by the Committee were suggested by Board and Faculty members.

The Committee determined at its first meeting that all the documents, specifically including the October 1976 paper of Mr. Shepherd, should be made available to the outside theologians. This decision was made on the assumption of some that this outside evaluation first would be sought, and then the Committee would write its "statement and study paper" dealing with the issue in the light of these evaluations.

But during a subsequent conference, it was determined that as a Committee the group first would write its statement, and then would confer with the outside theologians. When Mr. Robertson indicated that he felt the need to seek the counsel of outside theologians for the sake of his own further evaluation of the subject, it was agreed by common consent that all members of the Committee would be free to confer with whomsoever they would.

In view of this decision, Mr. Robertson and Mr. Settle jointly submitted the major documents of the discussion to various noteworthy theologians of the Reformed community. In a covering letter dated October 9, 1979, a special notation called attention to the qualifications associated with Mr. Shepherd's October 1976 paper, indicating that it was being shared by authorization of the Board, that it originally was presented to the Faculty as a study paper, and that it had been modified at the points indicated by Mr. Shepherd's March 1, 1978 paper. Mr. Shepherd's qualifications regarding the paper as expressed to the Presbytery of Philadelphia also were noted.

Loyalty to the best interest of Westminster Seminary was seen in the content and tenor of the various responses, including comments offered by such noteworthy theologians as D. Martyn Lloyd-Jones, Roger Nicole, Fred Klooster, R. C. Sproul, C. Gregg Singer, G. I. Williamson, and others. Some were able to respond within the requested four-week period. Others needed a longer period of time.

In the meeting of the Committee on December 16-17, 1979, it was concluded that in the Committee's preliminary judgment the previous decision of the Board not to examine Mr. Shepherd's views any further was premature. The Committee stated that this decision arose from its own preliminary review of the materials on the subject of justification, and from the counsel provided by theological scholars whose evaluations had been requested by individuals of the Committee.

The Committee discussed at length whether it could proceed any further with its work of writing a "statement and study paper" on the doctrine of justification at Westminster Seminary apart from a more formal treatment of the views of Mr. Shepherd. It was determined to proceed with "Affirmations and Denials" on the subject of justification. Mr. Robertson wrote the first draft of this paper, and also provided comparisons with the expressions of Mr. Shepherd dealing with the same subjects. So the Committee set about doing its work.

*The Committee's Conclusions*

The constitution of this Committee as well as the differences of viewpoint with respect to its task virtually guaranteed divergent conclusions in form and substance. And so it was.

At the February 1960 meeting of the Board, a partial report was submitted by the Committee. As already noted, this report indicated that in the Committee's opinion the Board had acted prematurely in concluding its discussion of Mr. Shepherd's views. The Board responded to the Committee's request to consult with Mr. Shepherd for the purpose of determining more precisely his views on the doctrine of justification by indicating that the Committee had the right to confer with any Faculty member in carrying out its task.

A supplementary report also was presented jointly by Mr. Robertson and Mr. Settle at the same meeting of the Board. In this report, a statement of the issue before the Seminary was followed by a brief history of the discussion, including the opinions offered by several "outside theologians" that had responded to their request. These included the following statements:

> *D. Martyn Lloyd-Jones*:
> [Mr. Shepherd's] teaching is a subtle form of legalism and eventually is "another gospel."
>
> *Roger Nicole*:
> Shepherd does (especially in his latest paper "The Grace of Justification") deny very forcibly that he gives any place to good works in the ground of justification. But by including our good works in the way to justification, he countenances an approach which warrants the fear that

> his distinction will not be readily perceived by most who hear of it, and that a reversal may develop toward a doctrine of justification by works, which would approximate the error of Romanism.
>
> *William Hendriksen*:
>
> As I see it, we must choose between Shepherd's view and that of Paul.
>
> *Meredith G. Kline*:
>
> Professor Shepherd posits a simple equivalence between the national election of Israel and the individual election to eternal salvation, calls this one variety of election – the only kind that figures, according to Professor Shepherd, in what we may say about the historical realm – covenantal election, and concludes from the fact that elect national Israel became reprobate national Israel that covenantal election, wherever it is found, is losable.

Similar evaluations had been received from R. C. Sproul, Morton H. Smith, C. Gregg Singer, Charles Dunahoo, Iain Murray, and Edward L. Kellogg.

Earlier the communications of all those who found no basic error in Mr. Shepherd's formulations had been included in the materials sent to Board and Faculty members. These communications came from Fred Klooster, Pierre Courthial, and G. I. Williamson. According to Professor Klooster, the clarifications of Mr. Shepherd's March 1, 1978 paper helped to bring out the original intentions of the October 1976 paper more consistently and more clearly. In this light he concluded, "I do not consider the views expressed to involve 'a significant doctrinal error,' nor even 'a doctrinal error.' "

G. I. Williamson summarized his evaluation in the following paragraph:

> I must reiterate that on the whole I do not think that Mr. Shepherd is undermining the doctrine of justification by faith. To the contrary, I come away from the study of what he has written with the opposite impression. While I would therefore urge Mr. Shepherd also "for the cause of the kingdom, to seek less provocative language, and different means of argument, less open to misunderstanding," I would also join in commending him for the concern to develop a more adequate statement of the doctrine of justification by faith. And I certainly think that I have been enriched by his efforts thus far.

Due to the language barrier and the shortness of time resulting from an overseas mailing, Mr. Courthial was able to read only Mr. Shepherd's *The Grace of Justification.* He found no difficulty in approving the doctrine found in *this* text (emphasis is Mr. Courthial's).

After the February 1980 meeting of the Board, the "justification committee" continued to work on "Affirmations and Denials," with "comparisons" to Mr. Shepherd's statements provided by Mr. Robertson. In April 1980, the Committee met in Philadelphia and asked Mr. Shepherd and Dr. W. Robert Godfrey to confer with them concerning their response to the Committee's work. At that meeting, an analysis of Mr. Shepherd's "covenantal perspective" as it related to the doctrine of justification was presented based on a number of citations of the public statements of Mr. Shepherd. The response of Mr. Shepherd to this presentation is analyzed by a subsequent letter to the Committee from W. Robert Godfrey, who also was present at the meeting:

> As in the past, Shepherd protested, but failed to respond to the specific citations to show how his state-

> ments should be understood. Unless there is a clear, specific response from Shepherd, I believe that...one must conclude that Shepherd's position in this matter is confusing and erroneous.*

While it should be noted that Mr. Godfrey was before the Committee as a critic of Mr. Shepherd's position, it is nonetheless accurate that Mr. Shepherd offered no explanation of the specific citations provided. Despite repeated reference to Mr. Shepherd's various public statements, he only commented that he had not been understood.

The Committee then proceeded to go through their various "Affirmations and Denials," with occasional reference to the "comparisons" that had been prepared by Mr. Robertson. Particularly significant was Denial II.3: "We deny that justifying faith can be defined properly so that it virtually includes in its essence the new obedience that faith inevitably produces."

This Denial was of some significance in view of Mr. Shepherd's affirmation that if faith is receiving Christ it is also obeying his commands, and that the command to believe and the command to follow Christ doing as he commanded are not ultimately different answers to the question concerning how a man is to be justified (October 1976 paper, 9, 51; *Thirty-four Theses* 20, 22, 23).

This tension between the denial of the Committee and the previous statements of Mr. Shepherd was pointed out by the "comparison" column that had been prepared. Mr. Shepherd was asked if he would be willing to retract his earlier statements in view of the Committee's denial.

* Letter to the Board-Faculty Committee on Justification dated April 30, 1980.

Mr. Shepherd made no answer.

The question was put to Mr. Shepherd again, and the Committee awaited an answer.

Mr. Shepherd made no reply.

At this point Mr. Robertson indicated that he would have to conclude that Mr. Shepherd still held to his original formulations, even though affirming the Committee's denial.

The identical situation recurred with the next set of "Affirmations and Denials." Mr. Shepherd agreed to the Committee's formulations concerning the "causal priority" of God's justification of the sinner to the existence in him of any new obedience that is accepted judicially by God (Affirmation II. 4). Yet he failed to clarify his previous statements that new obedience is necessary to justification (*Thirty-four Theses* 21, 22, 23; October 1976 paper, 19, 26).

Mr. Ryskamp, acting as chairman, then requested that further remarks based on the "comparison" column which related Mr. Shepherd's statements to the Affirmations and Denials be held back until after the Committee had completed its review of the other Affirmations and Denials with Mr. Shepherd. The Committee never returned to the "comparisons."

Mr. Shepherd indicated that he could agree with all the Affirmations and Denials of the Committee. But the cloud of ambiguity still remained.

The real question before the Committee never had been whether or not Mr. Shepherd would affirm an orthodox statement on justification. He had consistently made that affirmation from the beginning. Instead, the real question was the relation of the controversial statements of Mr. Shepherd to his acknowledged avowals of orthodoxy.

By excluding a procedure which might confront this question in the final stages of its work, the "Justification Committee" assured the continuance of the controversy. No possibility of genuine resolution existed so long as the Committee report avoided an examination of the very ambiguities which had originated the controversy.

In the end, the Committee presented to the Faculty and Board of the Seminary a divided assessment. Three members supported a majority report favoring the document which ultimately became the "Westminster Statement on Justification," after significant modifications as recommended by the Faculty were approved by the Board. Two members favored a minority report which included "comparisons" which contrasted with Mr. Shepherd's formulations.

The seeds of this division lay in the divergent perspectives on the task of the Committee. Some members of the Committee had viewed their task to be the writing of a "Westminster Statement" that could affirm Westminster's unity on the doctrine of justification. The statement adopted by the majority of the Committee as modified by the Faculty corresponded to this purpose. It affirmed that Westminster Seminary was united in holding to the Reformed doctrine of justification by faith alone. Other members of the Committee understood their task to be the writing of a statement, in consultation with outside scholars, that addressed the issue still dividing the Seminary Board, the Faculty, and the student body.

The existence of a "majority" and a "minority" report, divided by the support of three members against two, testified to the disunity that remained. Yet interestingly, an unexpected kind of unity developed among some members of the Committee during the year in which its deliberations were carried out.

For in the end all three Board members who had served on the Committee voted in support of a motion to find adequate cause for the dismissal of Mr. Shepherd at the meeting of the Board at which their report was presented. Even though they were divided as to the form of this Committee's report, and even though the motion to find adequate cause for the dismissal of Mr. Shepherd failed, all three Board members who had served on the special Committee voted in May 1980 in favor of this motion for the dismissal of Mr. Shepherd.

## *7. The Commission on Allegations (May 1980 – November 1980)*

The five-man "Committee to Draw Up a Statement," also known as the "Justification Committee," concluded its work with a majority report favored by three and a minority report favored by two. At the meeting of the Faculty that reviewed the divergent reports of the Committee, a carefully prepared transcript of Mr. Shepherd's address titled "Reprobation in Covenant Perspective: The Biblical Doctrine" was offered for distribution so that the Faculty could be made more aware of the role of Mr. Shepherd's "covenant perspective" in the issue. The Faculty refused to receive this transcript because of Mr. Shepherd's protest that a written form of his address would not communicate his message adequately.

Mr. Robertson made the following motion:

> In response to the reports of the justification committee, the Faculty concludes that Mr. Shepherd's structure of argumentation as well as many of his distinctive formulations on the doctrine of justification almost certainly will mislead the church, particularly in the context of his distinctive "covenantal perspective." The Fac-

> ulty concludes that this evaluation applies to many of Mr. Shepherd's doctrinal statements both before and after the April 25, 1978 urging of the Faculty that he be careful to seek language less open to misunderstanding.

This motion was tabled.

Among a number of modifications suggested for the Committee's report, the Faculty determined to recommend the deletion of the entire section on "Affirmations and Denials" dealing with the "covenant concept" in relation to justification. It was this subject that earlier had been of primary concern to Meredith G. Kline in view of Mr. Shepherd's assertion that an individual elected by God according to the election of *Ephesians* 1 could become non-elect, despite the fact that the election of God stands fast. The argument of some members of the Faculty was that this matter had not been discussed in the Faculty, and therefore formulations on this subject had not reached adequate maturity.

At the decisive meeting of the Board in May 1980, the President suggested three courses that could be followed: The Board could exonerate Mr. Shepherd; it could find adequate cause for his dismissal; or it could establish a Commission on Allegations to determine if charges should be brought against him.

The motion was made that the Board find adequate cause for Mr. Shepherd's dismissal.

Mr. Ryskamp, who had served as chairman of the Committee to Draw Up a Statement, spoke in favor of the motion. He explained that he understood the motion in terms of the decision of a grand jury, finding "probable or reasonable cause" for an accusation, thereby setting the stage for a formal hearing.

The motion failed.

The third course of action, supported by the President, passed. A Commission on Allegations was established, consisting of seven members.

Although called a "commission," which gave some sense of progress in the resolution of the matter, this body had none of the powers normally associated with a "commission." It had no authority to resolve the issue on behalf of the Board.

The Commission membership included Theodore Pappas, Norman Hoeflinger, Joel Nederhood, and Calvin Cummings from the Board. Faculty members were W. Robert Godfrey, Robert B. Strimple, and Vern Poythress.

In its meetings from May through November of 1980, the Commission reached a consensus on the form that allegations should take. It was agreed that any one of seven allegations, "if substantiated, might justify the removal of a tenured Faculty member at Westminster."

Principal allegations, as developed by the Commission and presented with extensive citations from relevant materials, included the following:

(1) The allegation that Mr. Shepherd's presentation of the doctrine of justification is confusing to the degree that it inevitably will be misunderstood, and will appear to many as a position incompatible with Reformed orthodoxy.

In support of this allegation, it was noted that several members of the Faculty and Board, as well as noteworthy Reformed scholars, had concluded that Mr. Shepherd's formulations communicated error. Several actions of Board and Faculty warning Mr. Shepherd concerning his formulations also were quoted.

On the surface of the matter, this allegation would be difficult to dispute. The testimony of Board members, Faculty members, and "outside theologians" clearly had indicated that Mr. Shepherd was communicating error, however orthodox his intentions might have been.

(2) The allegation that Mr. Shepherd's distinctive view of the covenant is erroneous, leading him to posit that those elected by God according to the election of *Ephesians* 1 actually may become reprobate, and that the "branches to be cut off" in *John 15* first were savingly united to Christ.

(3) The allegation that Mr. Shepherd has affirmed erroneous as well as orthodox views on the doctrine of justification, and has not yet repudiated his erroneous statements. This allegation notes that Mr. Shepherd originally taught that works are the instrument of justification, and that subsequent modifications of language have not displayed adequately that he has repudiated this frame of thinking.

The Commission on Allegations completed this portion of its task by October 9, 1980. It then presented its work to Mr. Shepherd, requesting that he respond in person at a meeting of the Commission on November 3 and 4. Mr. Shepherd met with this Commission for approximately nine hours.

The Commission was divided four to three with respect to the conclusion to which the defense of Mr. Shepherd should bring them. The majority of four recommended that Mr. Shepherd be exonerated, noting that he continued to affirm the standards of the Seminary. It did not respond to the evidence that Mr. Shepherd was being understood as communicating error, as the first allegation proposed.

The minority of three offered two optional paths for the Board: that Mr. Shepherd be dismissed because key formulations of his position on justification and the covenant will continue to mislead; or that Mr. Shepherd be asked to resign, despite the praiseworthy character of his work, because his teaching substantially confuses. The minority report cited once more the many sources that had judged Mr. Shepherd to be in error as evidence that his formulations would mislead. The inadequacy of his responses during his meeting with the Commission also was cited.

At the meeting of the Board in November 1980, the motion to exonerate Mr. Shepherd lost by a tie vote. The motion presented by the minority also lost, by a vote of twelve to nine. After further discussion, a motion to exonerate with a further admonition to Mr. Shepherd that he take care regarding his formulations passed by a vote of thirteen to nine.

So for the third time Mr. Shepherd had been exonerated by the Board of Westminster Theological Seminary. His expressions were found to be in accord with Scripture and the Westminster Standards. The matter now at last was finally resolved.

Or so it seemed – once more.

## *8. Implications for Church Union and Unity (Fall 1977 – Fall 1981)*

For six years, Board and Faculty members of Westminster Seminary had made hardly any formal communication with the church at large about the "justification controversy." The Board had acted to allow its members to share the documents related to the discussion. Mr. Shepherd's relation to the Presbytery of Philadelphia of the Orthodox Presbyterian Church had evoked some response. But to a remarkable degree, the entire matter had been kept "in house." Hardly any religious journal had given the slightest indication that the issue was being discussed.

Was this circumstance good for the Seminary, the church, and the Gospel? The question could be debated.

Those who had concluded that Mr. Shepherd's expressions were erroneous or misleading with respect to the essence of the Gospel had tried numerous avenues of relief. Charges had been brought before Philadelphia Presbytery of the Orthodox Presbyterian Church on September 30, 1977, and the material on which charges were based had been excluded by the court. But even further, the Presbytery had reached beyond the material submitted, and in a rather sweeping declaration had said that Mr. Shepherd's October 1976 paper and any testimony based on it would not be admitted as evidence without Mr. Shepherd's consent (March 18, 1978 meeting). This decision was made even though the debate within the Seminary continued to be based on this particular document and the materials arising from it. It thus became very difficult to envision a manner in which a meaningful resolution of the case could be made. Since adequate resolution in the minds of his critics depended on retraction of erroneous or misleading statements being privately debated but now excluded from the court, any hope for a judicial solution to the problem became remote.

The matter was further complicated by the Presbytery's conclusion with respect to their discussion of the *Thirty-four Theses* of Mr. Shepherd. These formulations had been received by the Presbytery in the hope that their discussion might substitute for the further pursuit of charges. After a year's debate the Presbytery defeated by a tie vote a motion that the *Theses* be found in accord with Scripture and the *Confession.* It also defeated a motion that the *Theses* be found out of accord with Scripture and the *Confession.*

The Presbytery temporarily set up a new committee, charged

with studying other available papers as well as the *Thirty-four Theses.* But later the Presbytery determined that instead of continuing its investigation, it would refuse to consider further discussion of Mr. Shepherd's views except in the context of regular judicial proceedings. Although the Presbytery might have established a committee to determine on its behalf whether charges should be made, it placed the burden of responsibility on concerned individuals. Presbyters also were told not to distribute documents alleging doctrinal error unless they had followed the instructions of *Matthew* 18:15-18 and regular forms of Presbyterian church government.

From one perspective, this decision of Presbytery could be seen as creating a Catch-22 situation. Already the Presbytery had determined that charges must not be based on testimony arising out of the primary materials being discussed at the Seminary. Yet without question, the heart of the controversy was found in these excluded materials. But now the Presbytery might be perceived as saying that the next step of Mr. Shepherd's opponents must be the formal filing of charges.

But on what were the charges to be based? Mr. Shepherd had issued some controversial statements that could be regarded as being outside the Seminary discussion, such as the *Thirty-four Theses.* Yet the Presbytery's previous decision did have the effect of removing the primary historical and documentary framework of the issue from consideration by the court.

So from one perspective on the Presbytery's actions, the opponents of Mr. Shepherd's views would be caught in a rather perplexing dilemma, particularly if they felt a satisfactory solution to the problem could be reached only by Mr. Shepherd's retraction of the erroneous or misleading statements inherent in the various papers which had been defended by him over the past several years in the Seminary, and which he continued to defend. They could file no charges based on these papers; but they could not pursue the matter further apart from charges related to these same papers.

However, the decision of Presbytery could be understood from another perspective which might not create such serious difficulties. Since the example of *Acts* 15 presented a situation in which doctrinal error was discussed openly and resolved on principle rather than on the basis of personal charges of one individual against another, the "regular judicial proceedings" required by the Presbytery certainly could involve this approach.

Furthermore, the opponents of Mr. Shepherd could plead that the steps required in *Matthew* 18 already had been followed. Mr. Shepherd had been approached numerous times on an individual basis, and with one or two others present. The Presbytery had discussed the matter openly before the public for over a year, and the Seminary had released the major documents to the public. So from this perspective, the way was open to broader public discussion in accord with the developments recounted in *Acts* 15.

In the meantime, the Board of the Seminary was preparing to make a significant decision on the substance of the issue. On December 10, 1980, the Commission on Allegations would present its report.

In anticipation of this meeting, a communication to the Board was drafted and signed by fifteen individuals expressing their concern over Mr. Shepherd's formulations. After the Board proceeded to vote at this December 1980 meeting to terminate the issue by exonerating Mr. Shepherd, forty-five individuals signed a covering letter so that this previous communication to the Board might be distributed more widely as a means of informing the church at large of the seriousness of the situation now being faced.

This covering letter addressed to "Friends of the Reformed Faith" was signed by forty-five individuals from various ecclesiastical backgrounds. Signers included seven Board members (Everett Bean, Calvin K. Cummings, Donald C. Graham, W. Stanford Reid, Paul G. Settle, George D. Sinclair, and Murray F. Thompson, emeritus) and five Faculty members (W. Robert Godfrey, Meredith G. Kline, Robert P. Knudsen, Arthur W. Kuschke, and Leslie W. Sloat). In addition, Faculty members of other seminaries who had studied the various documents joined in sharing this material. They included Mariano DiGangi (Ontario Seminary); Roger Nicole and Meredith M. Kline (Gordon-Conwell Seminary); George W. Knight, III, Robert L. Reymond, and O. Palmer Robertson (having transferred to the Faculty of Covenant Seminary); and William J. Stanway (Reformed Seminary). Other individuals included Rev. Henry W. Coray, Dr. David Freeman, Rev. John P. Galbraith, Rev. Albert N. Martin, Rev. Iain H. Murray, Dr. C. Gregg Singer, Dr. Morton H. Smith, Dr. Douglas Vickers, and Dr. William Young.

The May 4, 1981 "letter of concern" was widely circulated, particularly among ministers of the Orthodox Presbyterian Church and the Presbyterian Church in America. The intention was to make this concern publicly known to the church, with the hope that Westminster Seminary might be called back to its clear commitment to justification by faith alone, and that the Gospel might be preserved in the church.

The Faculty of the Seminary was incensed by this action. Two communications were addressed to signers of the letter, making serious accusations. A statement by Richard B. Gaffin, Jr., was distributed widely, finding fault with the letter because of its failure to follow "orderly judicial proceedings." This statement was interpreted widely to mean that charges never had been filed against Mr. Shepherd, and therefore "orderly judicial proceedings" had not been followed.

The Board of the Seminary offered a more positive response to this letter. It established a "Visitation Committee" to prepare recommendations with a view to finally resolving the issue. In the meantime, the Board determined that Mr. Shepherd should not teach the required course in the curriculum dealing with the doctrine of justification in the Fall of the forthcoming academic year.

Meanwhile, the issue proved to have immediate bearing on questions of church union and unity. For the "joining and receiving" procedures between the Orthodox Presbyterian Church and the Presbyterian Church in America were just then at a crucial point. As votes in committee were being taken, the "justification issue" reached its controversial climax.

The PCA committee requested a special session with the OPC delegation on March 6, 1981. The significance of this single issue was discussed pointedly, with Mr. Shepherd present as a member of the OPC committee. In the meeting it was indicated that Mr. Shepherd's expressions on the doctrine of justification would not be acceptable to many in the PCA.

Mr. Shepherd concluded that he could not support the OPC's joining the PCA if his distinctive views were to be attacked. He therefore brought a minority report to the OPC General Assembly in June 1981. In this report, he recommended "that the OPC respectfully decline the invitation extended by the PCA to apply for membership in that denomination."

After prolonged debate, the OPC General Assembly failed by only a few votes to gain the necessary two-thirds majority to accept the invitation of the PCA. But the next morning the issue was brought up again. This time the motion to "join" the PCA achieved the necessary two-thirds vote by a narrow margin.

The issue also played a major role in the debates concerning the "joining and receiving" of the Orthodox Presbyterian Church at the corresponding General Assembly of the Presbyterian Church in America later that same month. A petition asking the Assembly to defer action on its invitation to receive the OPC for a period of three to five years was submitted by O. Palmer Robertson, Ben Wilkinson, Robert J. Ostenson, Frank Barker, Henry M. Hope, Jr., and William J. Stanway. Reasons given for the petition were that the OPC still was debating formulations on the doctrine of justification by faith, and that distinguished Reformed scholars such as Martyn Lloyd-Jones, William Hendriksen, Roger Nicole, Meredith G. Kline, Iain Murray, Philip E. Hughes, Morton H. Smith, C. Gregg Singer, W. Stanford Reid, R. C. Sproul, and others had indicated that the Gospel itself might be obscured in the debated formulations.

Dr. Clowney, a fraternal delegate of the Orthodox Presbyterian Church, appeared in the meeting of the Committee of Commissioners on Interchurch Relations to plead that the PCA proceed to issue its invitation to the OPC despite the "justification issue" that now was being brought to the attention of delegates. He made a similar plea in the opening moments of the Assembly as an expansion on the customary words of diplomatic greeting.

A lengthy debate was held on the issue of the reception of

the OPC. The "justification issue" was essentially the only matter discussed. Mr. Kenneth Ryskamp, who had served as chairman of Westminster Seminary's Committee to Draw Up a Statement, and who now served as the Chairman of Westminster's Board of Trustees, had been elected Moderator of this session of the PCA General Assembly. During the debate he relinquished the Moderator's chair and spoke vigorously in favor of the PCA's "receiving" the OPC. He informed the Assembly that he had voted for Mr. Shepherd's dismissal on more than one occasion, but that he favored proceeding with an invitation to the OPC. R. C. Sproul also spoke in favor of the reception of the OPC, although he stated that Mr. Shepherd ought to resign.

By special motion, Dr. Clowney was granted the privilege of the floor. He emphasized that never had there been any question at Westminster Seminary about the ground of justification – only the righteousness of Christ served as the ground of the sinner's justification. He assured the Assembly that the only problem was the distinctive manner in which Mr. Shepherd expressed himself. He informed the Assembly of a special conference that was to be held in the summer of 1981, noting that Mr. Shepherd had agreed to participate. J. I. Packer, R. C. Sproul, Roger Nicole, and Morton H. Smith, among others, would seek to help the Seminary resolve the issue.

The vote was taken, and the motion to defer action on issuing the invitation to the OPC failed by 192 to 347. A positive motion to extend the invitation to the OPC then passed by a significant majority. On the next morning, a further motion expressed the concern of the PCA over the issue of justification in the OPC, and assured the OPC that the PCA would pray for a "definitive resolution."

The issue then went before the presbyteries of the PCA for their approval. After several presbyteries had supported the reception of the OPC, the Presbytery of Mid-Atlantic of the PCA, meeting in September, defeated the motion to receive the OPC by a tie vote.

Of the twenty-five presbyteries of the PCA, sixteen eventually voted yes and nine voted no to the reception of the OPC. This tally meant that the motion had failed to receive the three-fourths majority of the presbyteries required by the *Book of Church Order* of the PCA.

Various factors were cited, to explain why nine presbyteries rejected the OPC while twenty-five PCA presbyteries voted unanimously to receive the Reformed Presbyterian Church, Evangelical Synod. But it is clear that the "justification issue" played a decisive role. Apart from this factor, the OPC almost certainly would have been received by the PCA.

But the issue was not yet over. Several months still remained before the Assemblies that might unite the various denominations would come together.

Perhaps somehow the justification issue could be dealt with so that a union still could be effected that would include the Orthodox Presbyterian Church along with the Presbyterian Church in America and the Reformed Presbyterian Church, Evangelical Synod.

## *9. The Removal of Mr. Shepherd (Spring – Fall 1981)*

It is not exactly clear what started the chain of events that led to Mr. Shepherd's removal in November 1981. He had been exonerated three times by the Board. He had been cleared of all allegations against him.

At the General Assembly of the Presbyterian Church in America meeting in June 1981, President Clowney had indicated his judgment that there was no theological problem with Mr. Shepherd's views. The problem was only with the way in which Mr. Shepherd expressed himself. President Clowney also had announced that Mr. Shepherd had agreed to join with J. I. Packer, Roger Nicole, R. C. Sproul, W. J. Stanway, Morton Smith, and others to discuss the doctrine of justification at a colloquium in August 1981.

But a letter to prospective participants subsequently indicated that Mr. Shepherd had determined not to participate in the colloquium and intended to seek other ways to establish the correctness of his position. The colloquium was cancelled.

Clearly the reassessment of Mr. Shepherd's theological position by President Clowney during the summer and early fall of 1981 played a critical role in Mr. Shepherd's removal. On October 9 he presented to the Visitation Committee a formulation of "Controversial Issues in the Teaching of Professor Shepherd." This report in revised form (dated November 11, 1981) was sent to the full Board and subsequently made available to the public. The revised form consisted of twenty-two pages criticizing Mr. Shepherd's formulations.

After listening to some forty hours of Mr. Shepherd's most recent classroom lectures, President Clowney concluded that his views "differ from our Confessional standards and appear to threaten significant doctrinal positions" (November 11, 1981 paper, 7). He noted that "his views of the covenant as they are now being presented... raise other issues that put the justification discussion in a broader setting" (7). He observed that if he felt the "present crisis of confidence" were limited to "misunderstandings of Professor Shepherd's views," he would feel compelled to oppose any suggestion of resignation or dismissal (7). Instead, he found "views" that were "controversial" in the sense that they "differ from our Confessional standards" (7).

President Clowney's critique centered on the distinctive formulations concerning the covenant promoted by Mr. Shepherd. As early as the Downingtown Conference in 1978 this issue had surfaced with Mr. Shepherd's statement that a person could "lose" his justification, since Scripture presented justification only in the context of a covenant-justification which could be reversed. Meredith G. Kline's critiques in 1979 and 1980 also had indicated problems with Mr. Shepherd's covenant "dialectic." The Committee to Draw Up a Statement had summarized "Affirmations and Denials" on the relation of justification to a proper view of the covenant, although the Faculty subsequently had recommended the deletion of this section from the report. The Commission on Allegations also had concentrated on problems associated with Mr. Shepherd's "covenant perspective."

Now President Clowney concluded that Mr. Shepherd's formulations on the covenant communicated views that differed from the Confessional standards of the Seminary. His paper provided a rationale for removal that centered on the communication of views that appeared to threaten significant doctrinal positions in Mr. Shepherd's formulations.

In the context of this paper as presented to the Visitation Committee, the Executive Committee of the Board determined that Mr. Shepherd first should be suspended and then removed from his teaching position at Westminster Seminary. Their recommendation was to be presented at the November 1981 meeting of the Board.

The position now taken by Mr. Clowney was discussed at

length in Faculty meetings. A few days before the Board convened to consider the recommendation of the Executive Committee that Mr. Shepherd be removed, the Faculty passed a motion, with the support of Mr. Clowney, affirming its judgment that Mr. Shepherd's system of theology was *not* out of accord with Scripture and the *Confession.*

This most recent motion passed by the Faculty regarding Mr. Shepherd's views was reported to the Board, along with the recommendation from the Executive Committee, that he be removed, at a special meeting on November 20, 1981. Mr. Shepherd defended himself against the allegations criticizing his theology in Mr. Clowney's paper. Mr. Clowney responded once more with a critique of Mr. Shepherd's formulations.

The vote in the Board favoring the removal of Mr. Shepherd was thirteen to eight. According to the charter of the Seminary, a majority of total Board membership was necessary for removal, which was exactly thirteen votes.

This Board meeting also received a strong criticism of those individuals who had signed the May 4, 1981 letter to "Friends of the Reformed Faith." The Visitation Committee asked for the resignation from the Board and Faculty of the signers who refused to apologize. The Committee's recommendation was modified by the Board so that signers were asked to consider what damage they may have done to the Seminary and Mr. Shepherd, and to make all possible amends.

The Board then authorized the Executive Committee to draw up a statement expressing to the public its reasons for the removal of Mr. Shepherd. A statement was adopted by the Executive Committee on the day following the Board's decision to remove Mr. Shepherd. It noted (1) that Mr. Shepherd is removed; (2) that removal was necessary for the best interests of the Seminary; (3) that the Board was making no judgment whether Mr. Shepherd's views as such contravened any element of the system of doctrine taught by the Westminster Standards; (4) that too many people had concluded that in some qualified manner Mr. Shepherd's teaching appeared to contradict the Standards; (5) that this conclusion was caused by a combination of factors, including the indiscretions of the Board and of others, allegations that were at times one-sided, "deep inherent problems in the structure and the particular formulations of Mr. Shepherd's views," and Mr. Shepherd's manner of criticizing opponents; (6) that the matter appeared unresolvable; (7) that the Seminary must distance itself from the controversy by removing Mr. Shepherd; and (8) that the Seminary pledged itself to make clear the grounds for its removal action in order to protect Mr. Shepherd's name.

Because of the widespread reaction which this explanation of the Executive Committee created, some aspects of their statement need to be noted.

First of all, the substance of the statement by the Executive Committee actually originated prior to the action of the Board. A statement had been presented to an earlier Faculty meeting, and this statement was brought to the meeting of the Executive Committee. For this reason it should not be surprising that the statement by the Executive Committee may not have reflected accurately the sentiments of the Board itself in its dismissal action.

According to their own testimony, several Board members voted for Mr. Shepherd's dismissal because they judged his formulations to be in error. Particularly in light of the paper presented and defended before the Board by President Clowney, it is very likely that a majority of the Board at that meeting voted for Mr. Shepherd's dismissal because they had concluded that his formulations were continuing to communicate views differing from the Confessional standards of the Seminary.

But the "Removal Statement" of the Executive Committee did not clearly accent the doctrinal reasons for the removal, even though recognition of the theological problem was clearly present in the statement. One reason for the removal was stated to be the "deep inherent problems in the structure and the particular formulations of Mr. Shepherd's views." This assessment is as radical in its implications as the most stringent critic of Mr. Shepherd's theology could propose. Mr. Shepherd's "views" on the cardinal doctrine of justification have "deep inherent problems." This analysis goes even further in its critique than the April 1978 evaluation of the Faculty that "Mr. Shepherd's structure of argumentation seems bound to create misunderstanding." Deep problems are inherent in Mr. Shepherd's theology about justification and the covenant.

But this theological analysis in the "Removal Statement" is overshadowed by the initial disclaimer that the Board "makes no judgment whether Mr. Shepherd's views as such contradict or contravene any element in the system of doctrine taught by the Westminster Standards." His views and particular formulations on the doctrine of justification have deep inherent problems, but no judgment is made as to whether his views contradict the Westminster Standards.

Of course, these two statements cannot stand beside one another – unless it is to be assumed that the Westminster Standards are so ambiguous in their formulation of the doctrine of justification by faith alone that its latitude allows for views that possess "deep inherent problems."

It must be questioned whether the "Removal Statement" of the Executive Committee properly communicated the action or the sentiment of the Board. Although formal charges were not drawn up, the evidence points to the fact that Mr. Shepherd's formulations were judged by the Board as continuing to communicate views that differed from the doctrinal standards of the Seminary. Although other matters of a secondary nature had to be considered by the Board in its decision to release Mr. Shepherd, the ultimate issue focused on the views that his formulations were communicating.

The conclusion of numerous theological scholars of international repute make it self-evident that in these people's judgment Mr. Shepherd's mode of expression was communicating error. Although the Board may have desired to stop short of declaring Mr. Shepherd himself to be a heretic, his formulations were viewed as seriously misleading.

Only nine days before the Board met, the President of the Seminary had submitted a twenty-two page paper arguing that Mr. Shepherd's views differed "from the Confessional standards of the Seminary" and appeared "to threaten significant doctrinal positions." The adoption of a motion in the Faculty supportive of Mr. Shepherd three days before the meeting of the Board hardly could have altered the conclusion by the Board that Mr. Shepherd's views were seriously misleading.

On November 25, 1981, a news release from the Seminary announced Mr. Shepherd's removal. The statement continued the same impressions conveyed by the "Removal Statement" of the Executive Committee, although it did note that the Board had provided for a "full hearing." Mr. Shepherd was dismissed as of January 1, 1982.

The signers of the May 4, 1981 letter that had conveyed to

the public their concern over Mr. Shepherd's position received the first place of prominence in this news release. Even before the reasons for the removal action had been developed, it was noted that signers had been asked "to consider the possible damage caused by the letter to Shepherd and Westminster Seminary and to make all possible amends." The inference left by this news release was that the critics of Mr. Shepherd, characterized as making "one-sided allegations," were the ones who had provided the primary rationale for Mr. Shepherd's dismissal.

The impression that doctrinal reasons did not provide the basis for Mr. Shepherd's removal was reinforced before the student body of Westminster Seminary by an explanation of President Clowney on the day the press release was made available to the public. According to a letter widely circulated by a group of students present at the meeting, President Clowney "stressed repeatedly" that Mr. Shepherd was within the bounds of Reformed orthodoxy (letter to "Fellow Students and Alumni" dated December 14, 1981, and signed by seventeen students, 1). This letter also reported that President Clowney repeatedly stressed the exemplary conduct of Mr. Shepherd, while offering "pointed criticisms" of the signers of the May 4, 1981 letter (4).

These same positions with respect to the removal were made broadly available to the public by an alumni letter from President Clowney on December 29, 1981. Mr. Clowney underscored once more that Mr. Shepherd was not removed for doctrinal reasons. In the materials offered, stringent criticisms were directed against signers of the May 4, 1981 letter by Samuel T. Logan, Jr., Director of Studies at Westminster.

In this climate, it is not surprising that the press, in dependence on the Seminary's news releases, stressed this perspective. Westminster Seminary had removed a distinguished professor of systematic theology for something other than doctrinal reasons. Largely because of pressures brought by critics, Mr. Shepherd was released. (See *The Banner*, December 28, 1981, 6; *The Presbyterian Journal*, December 9, 1981, 4f; *Covenanter Witness*, February 1982, 19.)

Neither is it surprising that Mr. Shepherd would offer a challenge to the Board's action. Three times he had been exonerated of doctrinal error. Then he was "removed," primarily on the basis of a paper alleging serious doctrinal error by the President, even though the President himself subsequently supported the Faculty's affirmation that Mr. Shepherd's system of theology was not out of accord with Scripture and the *Confession.*

## *10. Challenge, Response, and Continuation*

### *Challenge*

Mr. Shepherd understandably challenged his dismissal by the Board at Westminster Seminary. He notified the Board that he wished a full hearing as the Constitution of the Seminary provided. He indicated that he had engaged legal counsel.

### *Response*

It therefore became the obligation of the Board to defend its action in dismissing Mr. Shepherd. This defense is summarized in a paper titled "Reasons and Specifications Supporting the Action of the Board of Trustees in Removing Professor Shepherd Approved by the Executive Committee of the Board," and dated February 26, 1982. This paper is most significant, particularly in that it appears to be the final statement of the

Seminary on the matter of the reason for Mr. Shepherd's removal. In an earlier press release, the Executive Committee of the Board had pledged itself to make public the true reason for Mr. Shepherd's removal.

This paper is eighteen pages in length. It contains ten pages reviewing the history of the controversy, and eight pages of theological critique of Mr. Shepherd's position. Several factors may be noted about the paper:

(1) The paper early affirms: "Since the Board did not remove Mr. Shepherd on the ground of demonstrated error in his teaching, charges of such errors, together with specifications, obviously would not be appropriate" (1) .

At first this statement would appear to dismiss altogether the question of doctrinal substance as a basis for Mr. Shepherd's removal. But even a cursory glance at the remainder of the paper, particularly the section titled "Problematics in Mr. Shepherd's Views," indicates that doctrinal substance actually was at the root of his removal.

(2) The first section of the paper summarizes the reasons for removal. After seven years of earnest study and debate, the Board had become convinced that Mr. Shepherd's teaching regarding justification, the covenant, and related themes "is not clearly in accord with the teaching of Scripture as it is summarized in the system of doctrine contained in the Westminster Standards" (2).

Immediately it becomes plain that doctrine as a matter of fact was the reason for Mr. Shepherd's removal. Although formal charges of doctrinal error may not have been presented, the substance of a significant doctrinal issue lay behind the entire matter.

(3) The historical tracing of the major events of the contro-

versy in the paper is useful and basically accurate, although it omits any reference to the Downingtown Conference, to the deletion of "Affirmations and Denials" regarding justification in relation to the covenant in the "Westminster Statement on Justification," or to the minority report of the Committee to Draw Up a Statement. The effect of these omissions is to give the impression that the question of Mr. Shepherd's "covenant perspective" arose only with his most recent lecture materials.

(4) The heart of this paper is found in the section titled "Problematics in Mr. Shepherd's Views" (11-18). Three problematic areas are specified. In each case, Mr. Shepherd's distinctive formulations are set over against the theology of the Westminster Standards.

First, the relation of works to faith is discussed. The report notes that in Mr. Shepherd's covenantal perspective the role of faith alone as instrument of justification is not adequately presented: "The confessional emphasis on faith as the alone instrument of justification is muted in [Mr. Shepherd's] 'covenant dynamic' accent. The Westminster Standards emphasize faith alone, not merely in contrast to self-righteous works, but in contrast to all that we might do" (12).

In essence, this critique says that Mr. Shepherd's formulations fail to promote an understanding of justification by faith alone. While the technical language of the report may tend to soften this criticism, its radical nature is nonetheless present. With all the refinements and modifications developed over seven years of intensive debate and discussion, this 1982 evaluation of the Executive Committee of the Board indicates that in their judgment Mr. Shepherd still stood where he had started in 1975. He may not so explicitly call works the "instrument" of justification as he did originally. But his most recent formulations communicate this same concept.

It is significant that the report appeals to Mr. Shepherd's original October 1976 paper among other sources to establish his view of the relation of good works to justification (12). That appeal supports the position that Mr. Shepherd's later statements continue to be consistent with this earlier paper. It also indicates that in the Executive Committee's judgment, Mr. Shepherd's effort to "distance" himself from the October 1976 paper must not be understood as a repudiation of the formulations found in that earlier work.

Second, the distinction between the covenant of works and the covenant of grace is analyzed. The report concludes that Mr. Shepherd's view contrasts with the covenantal structure of the Westminster Standards: "Mr. Shepherd rejects not only the term 'covenant of works' but the possibility of any merit or reward attaching to the obedience of Adam in the creation covenant. He holds that faithful obedience is the condition of all covenants in contrast to the distinction made in the *Westminster Confession*.... The covenant of works was conditioned upon perfect, personal obedience. The covenant of grace provides the obedience of Jesus Christ and therefore does not have our obedience as its *condition* but requires only faith in Christ to meet the demand of God's righteousness" (15).

Essential to the system of theology in the Westminster Standards is the distinction between a covenant of works and a covenant of grace. In the original covenant, justification could come only as man himself responded to the covenant in obedience. In the covenant of grace, justification could come only as someone *other than* the sinner himself responded to the covenant in obedience. Faith alone then could receive a righteousness legally accounted to be the sinner's.

This report says that Mr. Shepherd's theology confuses this most basic covenantal structure by promoting a single response of obedience for man in all the covenants:

> By rejecting the distinction between the covenant of works and the covenant of grace as defined in the Westminster Standards, and by failing to take account in the structure of the "covenantal dynamic" of Christ's fulfillment of the covenant by his active obedience as well as by his satisfaction of its curse, Mr. Shepherd develops a uniform concept of covenantal faithfulness for Adam, for Israel, and for the New Covenant people. The danger is that both the distinctiveness of the covenant of grace and of the new covenant fullness of the covenant of grace will be lost from view and that obedience as the way of salvation will swallow up the distinct and primary function of faith (15).

This guardedly worded paragraph from the report essentially states that (1) Mr. Shepherd's covenant structure is different from that found in the *Westminster Confession*; (2) Mr. Shepherd posits that the required response of personal obedience as the way of covenant blessing is the same in the creative and redemptive covenants, in contrast with the distinction of responses found in the *Westminster Confession*; and (3) the distinctive role of "faith alone" may be swallowed up by the larger category of obedience in Mr. Shepherd's presentation.

Again, the radical character of this evaluation must be recognized. The report's assessment is phrased appropriately in careful language. But the conclusion still stands: Mr. Shepherd's concept of the covenant structure of Scripture differs significantly from the system of theology found in the Westminster Standards.

Third, the nature of assurance is discussed. In this case, the formulations of Mr. Shepherd once more are set over against the teaching of the *Westminster Confession*. The report states: "Mr. Shepherd's covenantal dynamic recasts the Confessional doctrine of assurance" (16). While the term "recasts" may be read as something less than "contradicts," the further discussion of this point by the report sets the teaching of Mr. Shepherd over against the *Confession* and catechisms. While Mr. Shepherd properly emphasizes the need of perseverance, and attempts to give full force to the threats of Scripture, "he fails to take account of the 'informational' aspect of assurance through the witness of the Holy Spirit, in and with the Word, that we are children of God (*Romans* 8:16; *WCF* XVIII; *LC* Q. 80)" (17). This "failure" of Mr. Shepherd's theology, set in contrast with the statements of Scripture and the Westminster Standards, refers to his view that men can know their election only within the context of the "covenant," which for Mr. Shepherd means that this election may be lost (16).

The report also explains: "From this same covenantal perspective, according to Mr. Shepherd, justification can be lost" (16). Significantly, the report appeals to the *Thirty-four Theses* of Mr. Shepherd, particularly *Theses* 21 and 23, to establish that Mr. Shepherd did in fact teach that justification could be lost.

The effect of this perspective on the question of assurance is clear. If the only assurance concerning election and justification that the sinner can know refers to a "covenantal election" or "covenantal justification" that may be lost, what confidence is left for the believer? It should be noted that the report is speaking not merely of an "assurance" that may be lost. Instead it is election itself, justification itself, that is lost.

The report is careful to say that Mr. Shepherd also affirms that the election of God may not be lost, for those whom God elects and justifies cannot lose their election or fall from a state of justification (16). It was precisely these kinds of counter-assertions that led Meredith G. Kline to write earlier of the "dialectic" in Mr. Shepherd's theology. According to Mr. Shepherd, the only election discussed in Scripture is "covenant election" which may become reprobation, and yet the election of God stands firm.

In a particularly insightful section, the report notes that the Westminster Standards speak of an "infallible assurance" that may be gained without extraordinary revelation. According to the report's analysis of the *Confession*, this knowledge is not produced by special revelation, although it is as "infallible" as knowledge produced by special revelation would be (18). This assurance that cannot fall stands over against that assurance that knows only an election and justification that may be lost in Mr. Shepherd's theology.

The report thus affirms that in the crucial areas of justification, the covenant, and assurance Mr. Shepherd stands counter to the Confessional documents of the Seminary. It may be that the dismissal of Mr. Shepherd was not based on the ground of "demonstrated error" (1). But an analysis of this report indicates that this denial refers only to the "formal" ground rather than the "material" ground of the dismissal. For the report delineates major areas of difference between the theology of Mr. Shepherd and the theology of the Westminster Standards.

The concluding page of the report summarizes and underscores once more the difference between the "distinctive system"(!) of Mr. Shepherd's theology and that found in the Westminster Standards. The report commends his desire to combat "easy-believism" and to give full weight to the warnings of Scripture. But it notes pointedly that to achieve these purposes "Mr. Shepherd would make obedience the central and embracing category for our response to God and thereby question the restrictions that the Reformed standards have put on the place and function of our good works" (18). The report proceeds to note that although Mr. Shepherd affirms a distinct function for faith, his concept of the "dynamic" of covenantal relation "effectively subordinates faith to obedience" and shifts the balance "in a sensitive area of great theological importance."

The final paragraph identifies this distinctive aspect of his thought as that which has been "the troubling factor in these seven years of controversy." It then concludes that although the Board has not judged that Mr. Shepherd's views are in error, it has come to the conviction that his views "are not clearly in accord with the standards of the Seminary" (18).

The challenge by Mr. Shepherd concerning his dismissal precipitated this response of the Executive Committee of the Seminary on behalf of the Board. It is difficult to know all the matters that developed in the process of this interchange. But after the report had been completed and presented to Mr. Shepherd, he withdrew his appeal for a hearing before the Board.

Thus the case was ended, so far as the Seminary was concerned. Since the appeal had been withdrawn, the report of the Executive Committee was not considered formally by the Board, although it had been distributed to its membership.

After Mr. Shepherd withdrew his appeal, the Executive Committee had to consider whether or not it would distribute publicly its "Reasons and Specifications" paper. It might have been argued that since the appeal had been withdrawn, it would not be necessary or appropriate for the report to be circulated.

But such a position would have been difficult to justify in view of the conclusions of the report itself. Only by shutting out its obligation to the church of Christ at large could such a position have been taken. For the "Reason and Specifications" report had indicated that Mr. Shepherd's formulations taught that justification was by works, and that election and justification could be lost. It could only be judged as a most serious act of irresponsibility if this evaluation had not been made known to the churches.

The Executive Committee determined on June 10, 1982, to release their paper, declaring publicly the theological reasons behind their decision to dismiss Mr. Shepherd. Although some members of the Seminary community resisted this action, the paper was released.

*Continuation*

In May 1982 charges were presented respecting Mr. Shepherd once more before the Presbytery of Philadelphia of the Orthodox Presbyterian Church. These charges were filed with the Moderator and with the Stated Clerk of the Presbytery before the docket had been adopted.

At that same meeting of the Presbytery, Mr. Shepherd presented a request that he be dismissed to Classis Hackensack of the Christian Reformed Church. Although he had no call to a specific church, he had conferred with "the appropriate authorities of the Christian Reformed Church" prior to the meeting of Presbytery.

In setting up its docket, the Presbytery determined to consider the request of Mr. Shepherd for dismissal prior to considering the charges brought against him. While his dismissal was being discussed, an amendment was moved to the effect that Classis Hackensack be notified of the charges that had been filed against him. The majority of the Presbytery voted against this amendment.

A further order of business before the Presbytery had to do with the report of a special committee responsible for meeting with the signers of the May 4, 1981 letter addressed to "Friends of the Reformed Faith" who also were members of the Presbytery. The report of this committee was deferred to an adjourned meeting to be held the next month.

In June 1982 the Presbytery of Philadelphia held its adjourned meeting. Now the report of the committee to meet with the signers of the May 4, 1981 letter was heard.

This committee recommended that a new committee of three be elected. The new committee was given the responsibility of determining whether judicial charges ought to be directed against members of the Presbytery who had signed the May 4, 1981 letter, or any other individuals mentioned in the report.

At this point, an effort was made to share with the Presbytery a recent communication to the Board of Westminster Seminary from most of the signers of the original May 4, 1981 letter, as well as the Seminary Board's acknowledgment of this communication. Signers of the May 4, 1981 letter essentially had indicated that it was out of concern for the Gospel and the good of Westminster Seminary that they had issued their earlier letter. They also had defended their right to give public expression of concern over a basic doctrinal issue, particularly when numerous efforts had been made along various avenues to correct the matter previously.

The Board communication had responded to this letter by expressing appreciation for the loyalty shown to Westminster Seminary by the signers of the May 4, 1981 letter. The Board also noted the patience of the signers, and asked for their continued prayer.

The Presbytery refused to allow these most recent interchanges between the signers of the May 4, 1981 "letter of concern" and the Board of Westminster Seminary to be distributed. A chief spokesman against the introduction of these materials was Mr. Norman Shepherd.

Mr. Shepherd had been dismissed by the Presbytery to the Christian Reformed Church the previous month. At that time, the Presbytery had refused to notify the Christian Reformed Church of the charges filed against him.

But now he returned to the Presbytery and was granted the privilege of the floor. Now he was allowed to speak for a motion that could lead to charges against his critics, without being liable to charges himself.

So the stage was set for continuation of the issue. Mr. Shepherd was transferred out of Philadelphia Presbytery before charges filed against him could be heard. He was received into the Christian Reformed denomination and commended to all its churches as a potential pastor, without notation that charges had been filed against him. He was allowed to return and speak in favor of a motion that could lead to charges against his opponents.

In February 1983 the special committee of the Presbytery of Philadelphia of the Orthodox Presbyterian Church provided signers of the May 4, 1981 letter in the Presbytery with a copy of formally prepared judicial charges against them, and offered to meet with the signers to discuss the matter. But when this committee of Presbytery met with signers of the May 4, 1981 letter, it stated that although it differed with many judgments involved in actions related to the sending of the May 4, 1981 letter, it had concluded that "judicial censure is not warranted." This conclusion was communicated to the members of presbytery in April 1983, just prior to the end of the two-year statute of limitations, so that individual members of Presbytery might have opportunity to file charges if they so desired. The Presbytery adopted this recommendation of the committee by a vote of sixteen to eleven. By this action, the judicial aspects of the issue in a significant sense were brought to a close. Tension also was relieved that could have been created if the Presbytery had implicated by charges noteworthy leaders within and without the Orthodox Presbyterian Church.

## 11. *Causes of the Controversy*

What brought about these agonizing and seemingly hurtful disputes within the very womb of evangelical Christianity in America today? How could it be that those so close in theological background and commitment would find themselves so radically opposed on the central doctrine of justification?

Many false reasons have been cited as the source of the issue.

It has been said that misunderstanding of Mr. Shepherd's position is to blame for the controversy. If his opponents had been more careful in their evaluations, they would not have misread him.

Such a proposition begins to lose credibility after a certain point. As the circle of dissent from Mr. Shepherd's position broadens to include ever larger bodies of scholars, theologians, pastors, and laymen, the appeal to "misunderstanding" loses whatever convincing character it may have possessed.

As any pedagogue knows, the teacher is responsible to a great degree not only for what he says but for how he is heard. Communication has not been achieved until the hearer rightly understands the speaker.

It should not be suggested that Mr. Shepherd manifested incompetence in the area of communication skills. He continually demonstrated his ability as a trained scholar and a devoted theologian.

Yet in this case, evidence clearly indicates that whatever his intent, he communicated doctrine that many understood to contravene the teaching of Scripture and the *Westminster Confession.*

Another proposed explanation for the controversy has been the suggestion that Mr. Shepherd's theology represented a tradition of the faith of the Reformers different from the perspective prevalent among evangelical Presbyterians in America today. A rejection of his formulations on justification and the covenant would then signal a tragic narrowing of the Reformed tradition represented at Westminster Seminary and in American Presbyterianism. Evidence to support this analysis was found in the newly emerging "predominance" of the Presbyterian Church in America on the Board of Westminster Seminary.

A significant cultural distinction may be detected between the Scotch-English and the Dutch tradition of Calvinism as they have come to expression on American soil. It is true that the Presbyterian Church in America, representing the former of these traditions, has increased its representation on the Board of Westminster in recent days.

Yet it is difficult to establish a view of justification and the covenant rooted in the Canons of Dordt of the Dutch tradition that is different from that which may be found in the *Westminster Confession* and catechisms. The Reformers were united about the doctrine of justification. Their creedal statements reflect that unity. Although differences may be found at certain points, it is difficult to drive a wedge between these two traditions with reference to the doctrines of justification and the covenant.

Of course, if a difference of substance should have emerged, Westminster Seminary as a point of historical fact is committed to the formulations of the Westminster Standards. It is to these documents specifically and not to a broader Confessional base that the professors and Board members of Westminster Seminary are committed.

A head-count of the constituency of Westminster's Board with reference to their church affiliation dispels the theory that domination by the Presbyterian Church in America explains the conflict. At the time of the dismissal of Mr. Shepherd, the Board included seven members from the Orthodox Presbyterian Church, six members from the Christian Reformed Church, and six members from the Presbyterian Church in America. This proportioning hardly represents "PCA domination."

The wide spread of ecclesiastical background in the opponents of Mr. Shepherd's views also dispels the notion of a possible denominational "coalition" against him. Board and Faculty members opposing his views included representatives from the Orthodox Presbyterian Church, the Christian Reformed Church, the Reformed Church in America, the Canadian Presbyterian Church, the Reformed Church in the United States (Eureka Classis), the Presbyterian Church in America, and the Church of England.

A third explanation of the controversy has been made. It has been suggested that a "personality conflict" created the controversy. Strong individuals on either side encountered one another, with the inevitable result of an unending struggle.

It cannot be denied that strong personalities were involved in the issue. Persistence marked participants on each side of the controversy. But this phenomenon can neither be faulted in itself, nor blamed as the source of the problem. A matter of such crucial substance clearly justifies determination on the part of participants. Blame for the conflict must be found elsewhere.

It has been proposed with some vigor that the real blame for the controversy must lie at the doorstep of Mr. Shepherd's opponents. Their un-Christian procedures so marred the orderly process of evaluation that discussion of the theological substance of the matter became meaningless. By a prejudicial and premature calling forth of opinions from "outside theologians," and by a dissemination of one-sided allegations to the public, all hope of coming to a sympathetic understanding of Mr. Shepherd's legitimate concerns was destroyed. Instead, Mr. Shepherd became the public scapegoat of a seriously mishandled situation.

However, those opposed to Mr. Shepherd's views, and particularly the signers of the May 4, 1981 letter, had no guarantee that the broader community of the church would agree with them in their assessment of Mr. Shepherd's formulations. If their statement of the issue was prejudicial to Mr. Shepherd's views, then in time an evaluation of the primary documents of the discussion should make that fact evident to all. Interestingly, however, it has been Mr. Shepherd's opponents who have been most concerned that all the materials of the controversy be made available to the public, while at the same time recognizing the right and perhaps the necessity of Mr. Shepherd to retract any of his controverted statements.

In the final analysis, only the presence of an issue of substance can explain the controversy. Numerous factors have tended to conceal this reality. But this perspective alone provides an explanation of all the various elements involved in the controversy.

Not all theological disputes center on issues of substance. But this matter had substance from the beginning. Never has a view of justification and the covenant precisely like that of Mr. Shepherd's been proposed in the church. Indeed, many close parallels may be found. But as a man with distinctive academic gifts and qualifications, he has developed a unique perspective that represents new doctrinal formulations.

His formulations may be correct. His formulations may be in error. But they unquestionably have the earmarks of distinctiveness. As Dr. Roger Nicole analyzed the matter:

> In the final analysis it would appear that Shepherd is caught between the horns of a dilemma.
>
> Either his view is really consonant to what the Reformed tradition has generally understood to be the Biblical teaching on this subject, and here it would seem a pity that he should disturb the Church and the Seminary for the sake of a variant formulation that does not affect the substance of doctrine.
>
> Or, his view is really novel, and represents a significant departure from what has been taught at Westminster Theological Seminary for 50 years and in Reformed circles for 450 years. But then a much more thorough proof seems needed, than has been forthcoming thus

> far, to the effect that we must indeed modify our understanding of this tenet and make appropriate adjustments in order to remain obedient to the authority of the Bible.

It is somewhat difficult to capture all the nuances of a perspective that still is emerging. Yet an effort may be made to summarize the distinctiveness of Mr. Shepherd's formulations that generated this controversy:

(1) Justification has been perceived inadequately by the church through its use of a Roman legal model. The Biblical perspective requires that justification be understood in terms of the dynamic of the covenant model. The "covenant of *life*" must not be reduced to a legalistic courtroom setting, even when discussing specifically the doctrine of justification.

(2) Election has been viewed deficiently by the dominance of a static model of God's unchanging decrees. Since man cannot perceive the elect as God sees them, it is fruitless as well as misleading to assume this perspective. Instead, the church must view election as Scripture does, which is out of the dynamic of the covenant. God indeed elects unchangeably. But he nonetheless functions in the dynamic of the covenant. In this framework the movement from reprobation to election also opens the real possibility that God's elect may become reprobate.

(3) Church membership and the sacraments must be seen for what they really are. They define genuine positions and experience in the covenant of grace. Any lesser perspective on their significance mocks the divine ordinances and contradicts the clear teaching of many portions of Scripture. Baptism rather than regeneration marks the point of transition from death to life. But discontinuation in the covenant ordinances means damnation.

(4) Faith and its fruits never can be abstracted from one another, for to believe is to obey. As a consequence, the way of justification before God is the way of obedience, and obedience is the way of justification. The unity of man's salvation finds its realization in the dynamic of covenant living.

Time will uncover the ultimate consequences of Mr. Shepherd's distinctive formulations. But as novel perspectives on the Biblical teaching concerning justification, the covenant, the sacraments, and the relation of faith to works, they provided the catalyst for the current controversy. This issue was one of theological substance and not of incidental disagreements that could have been avoided.

Complicating the entire process was the relationship developed between the Seminary community and the church. Ecclesiastical approval for ministry depended on the evaluation of materials by the Presbytery. Seminary approval depended on evaluation of materials by the Board and Faculty. The church and the Seminary of necessity had to take into account the evaluations of one another.

Yet the two groups simultaneously were working with different sets of materials. Even as the Seminary was evaluating the October 1976 paper and a subsequent paper modifying four of its most controversial formulations, the Presbytery was determining not to admit this material as evidence for charges against Mr. Shepherd. The Presbytery eventually moved on to evaluate Mr. Shepherd's *Thirty-four Theses*, and in the end failed to pass a motion finding them in accord with Scripture and the *Confession.*

When considered by a select group of Faculty members at the Downingtown Conference, these *Theses* failed to provide a basis for unity, particularly when placed in the context of Mr. Shepherd's distinctive views on the covenant.

A partial reason for prolonging the controversy appears to reside in this distinction between the respective roles of Presbytery and Seminary. The Seminary had opportunity to make a more thorough analysis of Mr. Shepherd's distinctive formulations because of its access to a broader scope of materials. But their evaluation did not have the advantage of open and public discussion in which it would become apparent how Mr. Shepherd would be heard by the church at large.

On the other hand, the Presbytery restricted the scope of materials it would consider. By such an action, it closed the door to a most important avenue of relief for the opponents of Mr. Shepherd's views. He had propounded and defended for a two-year period certain doctrinal statements that never had been seen by the Presbytery. Although he made a general statement regretting their problematic nature, he never retracted anything in particular. The Presbytery, therefore, never was in a position to judge whether Mr. Shepherd's more recent formulations actually did represent a repudiation of the specific statements that were proposed to be of an erroneous or misleading nature.

At the same time, the general statement of regret made by Mr. Shepherd to the Presbytery hardly could be expected to satisfy Faculty and Board members who had heard him repeatedly defend the most controverted of his statements. A way of relief could have been found if Mr. Shepherd had retracted statements regarded as erroneous or misleading. But so long as one set of documents was being considered by the Seminary, and a different set of documents was being considered by the Presbytery, it was not likely that this step would be taken.

A third major cause of the controversy may be proposed. It has been identified by some as the ascendancy of "Biblical Theology" over Systematics.

Mr. Shepherd in his own mind had discovered a distinctive teaching on justification in *James.* He desired to allow *James* to speak with full canonical authority in the church. He did not want the formulations of Paul to mute the vital words of *James* that justification was "by works."

Mr. Shepherd also wished to give full weight to the warnings of Scripture concerning those who professed faith but did not live in obedience. Particularly the warnings of *Hebrews* needed to be given their proper place in a doctrine of justification, since this book insisted on a "holiness" without which no one could see the Lord.

The experience of elect Israel also needed a renewed emphasis in the modern church scene. Unquestionably Israel had been the elect of God. The distinctive words of *Deuteronomy* 7 clearly asserted that fact. Yet they had become "not-my-people," the reprobate among the nations. This distinctive message of Scripture needed to be given its proper role in the doctrine of justification.

It was in the framework of bringing together these various testimonies of Scripture that Mr. Shepherd developed his distinctive formulations. The older "order" of God's applying the benefit of Christ's redemption (the *ordo salutis*) needed reassessment in the light of this new data provided by "Biblical Theology." Systematics must now be "informed" by these new perspectives.

This ascendancy of "Biblical Theology" over Systematics could be hailed as a great triumph which would lead to renewal in a church permeated with the errors of "easy-believism." All the vitalities and distinctive insights of the Biblical Theologian could become the catalyst for compelling the church to rethink its dogmatic assumptions about "once saved, always saved" that too often lead to presumption.

The church can only rejoice over the discovery of fresh insights provided by the discipline of "Biblical Theology." Drawing out the distinctive emphases of the various portions of Scripture must inevitably enrich the church's appreciation of the variegated revelation of God to men.

But some reserve must be expressed on this subject. First, the Biblical Theologian must be very careful that his exegesis is correct as he deals with the various portions of Scripture. Secondly, the Biblical Theologian must emphasize the rich diversity and distinctive message of Scripture only in a framework in which he also recognizes the controls exercised by the unity of the whole of Scripture. In other words, the "progress" of revelation must always proceed with a full awareness of the final stages of the revelational process. For it must be remembered that the ultimate context of any particular Scripture is the totality of Scripture.

Mr. Shepherd was not altogether convincing with respect to his basic exegesis of certain portions of Scripture which have played a crucial role in the development of his new "Biblical Theology." He posited that justification had identical significance in the letter of *James* and in Paul's argument in *Romans* and *Galatians.* Yet even though he analyzed rather carefully the optional meanings of the word "to justify" in *James*, he never established that James meant specifically that the guilty, polluted sinner had all his sins forgiven "by works" and not merely "by faith." In this case, it would not be adequate to show that James used the term "justified" semantically to mean "declared to be just" rather than "demonstrated to be just." For the meaning of *justification* in Paul can be understood properly only in terms of the total context which deals with the way guilt is removed. In order to establish that Pauline "justification" is "by works," Mr. Shepherd would have to show that James' intention was to affirm that all the guiltiness of the polluted sinner is removed by the sinner's own actions – actions which in themselves at best are imperfect and sinful.

In a similar manner, when Mr. Shepherd asserted that Paul excluded only works done in an attitude of boasting and pride from the "way" of justification and did not intend to exclude also the "good works" done in faith by the regenerate as the "way" of justification, he had the obligation of establishing this point on clear exegetical grounds. Working in the context of history since the Reformation, he basically had a responsibility to answer the argument of John Calvin and others in their analysis of the scope of the "works of the law" excluded from justification by Paul. Calvin had argued quite convincingly that if Paul were excluding only boastful works from justification, then he would not have cited the Old Testament to show that if a person should do these very "works" he would be blessed with *life* (see John Calvin's treatment of *Galatians* 3:10, 13 in his *Institutes* III, ii, 19).

When Mr. Shepherd's exegesis of Paul is joined to his exegesis of James, the implication is that a man is justified by good works done in faith, although he is not justified by works done in prideful boasting. His ambiguous use of the phrase "obedience of faith" then serves as a means of communicating the idea that justification is by the *obedient acts* done in faith as well as by *faith*, which inevitably comes to expression in obedience to God.

Some have credited "Biblical Theology" with these "fresh insights" into the way of justification. But if the "distinctive" messages of Paul and of James both have been represented from a perspective that is not precisely true to their own message, then the "Biblical Theology" arising from these conclusions could not prove to be helpful to the church.

A close scrutiny also must be made of Mr. Shepherd's analysis of the teaching of *Deuteronomy*, *Ephesians*, and *Hebrews* on election, the covenant, and perseverance. Is it true that God's election of individuals under the new covenant actually is of the same sort as God's election of national Israel under the old? Do the typological limitations associated with national Israel's election continue in the individual election described in *Ephesians* 1? May a person elected by God according to the categories of *Ephesians* 1 lose his elected status just as the nation of Israel lost theirs in the historical event of the exile? Is the only election found in Scripture something that may be called "covenant election," referring to an election-in-covenant that may become reprobation?

Once more the appeal to the discipline of "Biblical Theology" must be weighed with care.

It is true that the distinctive emphasis of every portion of Scripture must be given full expression. Such a distinction in the progress of revelation with respect to divine election and reprobation is brought out by Geerhardus Vos when he notes that the doctrines of election and reprobation "are by preference viewed in the Old Testament as they emerge in the actual control of the issues of *history*. It is God acting in result of his eternal will, rather than *willing in advance of His temporal act* that is emphasized in the Old Testament stage of revelation."* This old covenant emphasis on viewing God's eternal decrees through the admittedly limited perspective of historical images may be contrasted with the greater emphasis of the New Testament on the "eternal background" of the same reality (*ibid.*).

In attempting to make relevant the significance of the movement from election to reprobation of Israel under the old covenant, Mr. Shepherd asserted that the individual elected according to *Ephesians* 1 also could become reprobate. But it must be questioned whether he has communicated adequately the progress of Scriptural revelation as described by Vos. Instead of letting the finalized revelation of the New Testament provide the framework for understanding the shadowy form of the Old Testament, it may be that Mr. Shepherd has allowed the typological forms of the Old Testament to exercise too much control over the manner in which the New Testament is to be read. As a consequence of this perspective on election, a corresponding perspective emerged in his development of the idea of a "justification" that actually could be lost.

The Biblical Theologian must not only describe accurately the distinctive message of the various portions of Scripture. He must also balance Scriptural diversity with Scriptural unity. The distinctive message of each portion of Scripture has as its final and definitive context the totality of the teaching of Scripture. In the end, portions of Scripture which deal most explicitly with the topic at hand must be given their full

*Geerhardus Vos, "The Biblical Importance of the Doctrine of Preterition" in *Redemptive History and Biblical Interpretation*, edited by Richard B. Gaffin, Jr., Presbyterian and Reformed Publishing Company, 1980, 413, emphasis supplied.

weight. The "shadows" of Old Testament Scripture must be interpreted in context of New Testament "reality." The obscurities of Scripture must be understood in the light of its more explicit teaching.

In view of these considerations, it may be inappropriate to credit the "fresh insights" of Biblical Theology in contrast to Systematics for originating this controversy. Only as exegesis functions accurately in describing the progress of revelation meaningfully in the context of the total message of Scripture may it properly be termed "Biblical Theology."

Professor John Murray of Westminster Seminary often spoke of the "razor's edge" that separated truth from error. He himself possessed a unique capacity to draw out the distinctive message of the various portions of Scripture without contradicting the unified testimony of the whole.

But the delicate art of exegesis can be spoiled by setting one statement over against another if an actual dialectic is created. The assertions of one text may be overstated so that an equivalent adjustment-in-error of many other texts may be required for maintaining "harmony" in Scripture.

For these and other reasons this controversy on justification has arisen in the church today. It is indeed painful to engage in such a vigorous debate on the central doctrine of justification.

But perhaps the controversy itself may be the means by which the church will clarify and deepen its thinking. Perhaps the church will be prepared for even more meaningful advances in testifying to the saving grace of Jesus Christ, who is "The Lord our Righteousness" (*Jeremiah* 33:16).

# Index

# Scripture Index

# The Crisis of Our Time

HISTORIANS have christened the thirteenth century the Age of Faith and termed the eighteenth century the Age of Reason. The present age has been called many things: the Atomic Age, the Age of Inflation, the Age of the Tyrant, the Age of Aquarius; but it deserves one name more than the others: the Age of Irrationalism. Contemporary secular intellectuals are anti-intellectual. Contemporary philosophers are anti-philosophy. Contemporary theologians are anti-theology.

In past centuries, secular philosophers have generally believed that knowledge is possible to man. Consequently they expended a great deal of thought and effort trying to justify knowledge. In the twentieth century, however, the optimism of the secular philosophers all but disappeared. They despaired of knowledge.

Like their secular counterparts, the great theologians and doctors of the church taught that knowledge is possible to man. Yet the theologians of the present age also repudiated that belief. They too despaired of knowledge. This radical skepticism has penetrated our entire culture, from television to music to literature. *The Christian at the beginning of the twenty-first century is confronted with an overwhelming cultural consensus – sometimes stated explicitly but most often implicitly: Man does not and cannot know anything truly.*

What does this have to do with Christianity? Simply this: If man can know nothing truly, man can truly know nothing. We cannot know that the Bible is the Word of God, that Christ died for his people, or that Christ is alive today at the right hand of the Father. Unless knowledge is possible, Christianity is nonsensical, for it claims to be knowledge. What is at stake at the beginning of the twenty-first century is not simply a single doctrine, such as the virgin birth, or the existence of Hell, as important as those doctrines may be, but the whole of Christianity itself. If knowledge is not possible to man, it is worse than silly to argue points of doctrine – it is insane.

The irrationalism of the present age is so thoroughgoing and pervasive that even the Remnant – the segment of the professing church that remains faithful – has accepted much of it, frequently without even being aware of what it is accepting. In some religious circles this irrationalism has become synonymous with piety and humility, and those who oppose it are denounced as rationalists, as though to be logical were a sin. Our contemporary anti-theologians make a contradiction and call it a Mystery. The faithful ask for truth and are given Paradox and Antinomy. If any balk at swallowing the absurdities of the anti-theologians who teach in the seminaries or have graduated from the seminaries, they are frequently marked as heretics or schismatics who seek to act independently of God.

There is no greater threat facing the church of Christ at this moment than the irrationalism that now controls our entire culture. Totalitarianism, guilty of tens of millions of murders – including those of millions of Christians – is to be feared, but not nearly so much as the idea that we do not and cannot know the literal truth. Hedonism, the popular philosophy of

America, is not to be feared so much as the belief that logic – that "mere human logic," to use the religious irrationalists' own phrase – is futile. The attacks on truth, on knowledge, on propositional revelation, on the intellect, on words, and on logic are renewed daily. But note well: The misologists – the haters of logic – use logic to demonstrate the futility of using logic. The anti-intellectuals construct intricate intellectual arguments to prove the insufficiency of the intellect. Those who deny the competence of words to express thought use words to express their thoughts. The proponents of poetry, myth, metaphor, and analogy argue for their theories by using literal prose, whose competence – even whose possibility – they deny. The anti-theologians use the revealed Word of God to show that there can be no revealed Word of God – or that if there could, it would remain impenetrable darkness and Mystery to our finite minds.

## *Nonsense Has Come*

Is it any wonder that the world is grasping at straws – the straws of experientialism, mysticism, and drugs? After all, if people are told that the Bible contains insoluble mysteries, then is not a flight into mysticism to be expected? On what grounds can it be condemned? Certainly not on logical grounds or Biblical grounds, if logic is futile and the Bible unknowable. Moreover, if it cannot be condemned on logical or Biblical grounds, it cannot be condemned at all. If people are going to have a religion of the mysterious, they will not adopt Christianity: They will have a genuine mystery religion. The popularity of mysticism, drugs, and religious experience is the logical consequence of the irrationalism of the present age. There can and will be no Christian reformation – and no restoration of a free society – unless and until the irrationalism of the age is totally repudiated by Christians.

## *The Church Defenseless*

Yet how shall they do it? The official spokesmen for Christianity have been fatally infected with irrationalism. The seminaries, which annually train thousands of men to teach millions of Christians, are the finishing schools of irrationalism, completing the job begun by the government schools and colleges. Most of the pulpits of the conservative churches (we are not speaking of the obviously apostate churches) are occupied by graduates of the anti-theological schools. These products of modern anti-theological education, when asked to give a reason for the hope that is in them, can generally respond with only the intellectual analogue of a shrug – a mumble about Mystery. They have not grasped – and therefore cannot teach those for whom they are responsible – the first truth: "And you shall know the truth." Many, in fact, explicitly contradict Christ, saying that, at best, we possess only "pointers" to the truth, or something "similar" to the truth, a mere analogy. Is the impotence of the Christian church a puzzle? Is the fascination with Pentecostalism, faith healing, Eastern Orthodoxy, and Roman Catholicism – all sensate and anti-intellectual religions – among members of Christian churches an enigma? Not when one understands the pious nonsense that is purveyed in the name of God in the religious colleges and seminaries.

## *The Trinity Foundation*

The creators of The Trinity Foundation firmly believe that theology is too important to be left to the licensed theologians

– the graduates of the schools of theology. They have created The Trinity Foundation for the express purpose of teaching the faithful all that the Scriptures contain – not warmed over, baptized, Antichristian philosophies. Each member of the board of directors of The Trinity Foundation has signed this oath: "I believe that the Bible alone and the Bible in its entirety is the Word of God and, therefore, inerrant in the autographs. I believe that the system of truth presented in the Bible is best summarized in the *Westminster Confession of Faith.* So help me God."

The ministry of The Trinity Foundation is the presentation of the system of truth taught in Scripture as clearly and as completely as possible. We do not regard obscurity as a virtue, nor confusion as a sign of spirituality. Confusion, like all error, is sin, and teaching that confusion is all that Christians can hope for is doubly sin.

The presentation of the truth of Scripture necessarily involves the rejection of error. The Foundation has exposed and will continue to expose the irrationalism of the present age, whether its current spokesman be an existentialist philosopher or a professed Reformed theologian. We oppose anti-intellectualism, whether it be espoused by a Neo-orthodox theologian or a fundamentalist evangelist. We reject misology, whether it be on the lips of a Neo-evangelical or those of a Roman Catholic Charismatic. We repudiate agnosticism, whether it be secular or religious. To each error we bring the brilliant light of Scripture, proving all things, and holding fast to that which is true.

## *The Primacy of Theory*

The ministry of The Trinity Foundation is not a "practical" ministry. If you are a pastor, we will not enlighten you on how to organize an ecumenical prayer meeting in your community or how to double church attendance in a year. If you are a homemaker, you will have to read elsewhere to find out how to become a total woman. If you are a businessman, we will not tell you how to develop a social conscience. The professing church is drowning in such "practical" advice.

The Trinity Foundation is unapologetically theoretical in its outlook, believing that theory without practice is dead, and that practice without theory is blind. The trouble with the professing church is not primarily in its practice, but in its theory. Churchgoers and teachers do not know, and many do not even care to know, the doctrines of Scripture. Doctrine is intellectual, and churchgoers and teachers are generally anti-intellectual. Doctrine is ivory tower philosophy, and they scorn ivory towers. The ivory tower, however, is the control tower of a civilization. It is a fundamental, theoretical mistake of the "practical" men to think that they can be merely practical, for practice is always the practice of some theory. The relationship between theory and practice is the relationship between cause and effect. If a person believes correct theory, his practice will tend to be correct. The practice of contemporary Christians is immoral because it is the practice of false theories. It is a major theoretical mistake of the "practical" men to think that they can ignore the ivory towers of the philosophers and theologians as irrelevant to their lives. Every action that "practical" men take is governed by the thinking that has occurred in some ivory tower – whether that tower be the British Museum; the Academy; a home in Basel, Switzerland; or a tent in Israel.

## *In Understanding Be Men*

It is the first duty of the Christian to understand correct theory – correct doctrine – and thereby implement correct practice. This order – first theory, then practice – is both logical and Biblical. It is, for example, exhibited in Paul's *Epistle to the Romans,* in which he spends the first eleven chapters expounding theory and the last five discussing practice. The contemporary teachers of Christians have not only reversed the Biblical order, they have inverted the Pauline emphasis on theory and practice. The virtually complete failure of the teachers of the professing church to instruct believers in correct doctrine is the cause of the misconduct and spiritual and cultural impotence of Christians. The church's lack of power is the result of its lack of truth. The *Gospel* is the power of God, not religious experiences or personal relationships. The church has no power because it has abandoned the Gospel, the good news, for a religion of experientialism. Twentieth-first-century American churchgoers are children carried about by every wind of doctrine, not knowing what they believe, or even if they believe anything for certain.

The chief purpose of The Trinity Foundation is to counteract the irrationalism of the age and to expose the errors of the teachers of the church. Our emphasis – on the Bible as the sole source of knowledge, on the primacy of truth, on the supreme importance of correct doctrine, and on the necessity for systematic and logical thinking – is almost unique in Christendom. To the extent that the church survives – and she will survive and flourish – it will be because of her increasing acceptance of these basic ideas and their logical implications.

We believe that The Trinity Foundation is filling a vacuum in Christendom. We are saying that Christianity is intellectually defensible – that, in fact, it is the only intellectually defensible system of thought. We are saying that God has made the wisdom of this world – whether that wisdom be called science, religion, philosophy, or common sense – foolishness. We are appealing to all Christians who have not conceded defeat in the intellectual battle with the world to join us in our efforts to raise a standard to which all men of sound mind can repair.

The love of truth, of God's Word, has all but disappeared in our time. We are committed to and pray for a great instauration. But though we may not see this reformation in our lifetimes, we believe it is our duty to present the whole counsel of God, because Christ has commanded it. The results of our teaching are in God's hands, not ours. Whatever those results, his Word is never taught in vain, but always accomplishes the result that he intended it to accomplish. Professor Gordon H. Clark has stated our view well:

"There have been times in the history of God's people, for example, in the days of Jeremiah, when refreshing grace and widespread revival were not to be expected: The time was one of chastisement. If this twentieth century is of a similar nature, individual Christians here and there can find comfort and strength in a study of God's Word. But if God has decreed happier days for us, and if we may expect a world-shaking and genuine spiritual awakening, then it is the author's belief that a zeal for souls, however necessary, is not the sufficient condition. Have there not been devout saints in every age, numerous enough to carry on a revival? Twelve such persons are plenty. What distinguishes the arid ages from the period of the Reformation, when nations were moved as they had not been since Paul preached in Ephesus, Corinth, and Rome, is the latter's fullness of knowledge of God's Word. To echo an early Reformation thought, when the ploughman and the garage attendant know the Bible as well as the theologian does, and know it better than some contemporary theologians, then the desired awakening shall have already occurred."

In addition to publishing books, the Foundation publishes a monthly newsletter, *The Trinity Review.* Subscriptions to *The Review* are free to U.S. addresses; please write to the address on the order form to become a subscriber. If you would like further information or would like to join us in our work, please let us know.

The Trinity Foundation is a non-profit foundation, tax exempt under section 501 (c)(3) of the Internal Revenue Code of 1954. You can help us disseminate the Word of God through your tax-deductible contributions to the Foundation.

JOHN W. ROBBINS

# Intellectual Ammunition

THE Trinity Foundation is committed to bringing every philosophical and theological thought captive to Christ. The books listed below are designed to accomplish that goal. They are written with two subordinate purposes: (1) to demolish all non-Christian claims to knowledge; and (2) to build a system of truth based upon the Bible alone.

## Philosophy

*Ancient Philosophy*
Gordon H. Clark — Trade paperback $24.95

This book covers the thousand years from the Pre-Socratics to Plotinus. It represents some of the early work of Dr. Clark – the work that made his academic reputation. It is an excellent college text.

*Behaviorism and Christianity*
Gordon H. Clark — Trade paperback $5.95

*Behaviorism* is a critique of both secular and religious behaviorists. It includes chapters on John Watson, Edgar S. Singer, Jr., Gilbert Ryle, B. F. Skinner, and Donald MacKay. Clark's refutation of behaviorism and his argument for a Christian doctrine of man are unanswerable.

*A Christian Philosophy of Education* Hardback $18.95
Gordon H. Clark Trade paperback $12.95

The first edition of this book was published in 1946. It sparked the contemporary interest in Christian schools. In the 1970s, Dr. Clark thoroughly revised and updated it, and it is needed now more than ever. Its chapters include: The Need for a World-View; The Christian World-View; The Alternative to Christian Theism; Neutrality; Ethics; The Christian Philosophy of Education; Academic Matters; and Kindergarten to University. Three appendices are included: The Relationship of Public Education to Christianity; A Protestant World-View; and Art and the Gospel.

*A Christian View of Men and Things* Hardback $29.95
Gordon H. Clark Trade paperback $14.95

No other book achieves what *A Christian View* does: the presentation of Christianity as it applies to history, politics, ethics, science, religion, and epistemology. Dr. Clark's command of both worldly philosophy and Scripture is evident on every page, and the result is a breathtaking and invigorating challenge to the wisdom of this world.

*Clark Speaks from the Grave*
Gordon H. Clark Trade paperback $3.95

Dr. Clark chides some of his critics for their failure to defend Christianity competently. *Clark Speaks* is a stimulating and illuminating discussion of the errors of contemporary apologists.

*Ecclesiastical Megalomania:*
*The Economic and Political Thought*
*of the Roman Catholic Church*
John W. Robbins Hardback $21.95

This detailed and thorough analysis and critique of the social teaching of the Roman Church-State is the only such book available by a Christian economist and political philosopher. The book's conclusions reveal the Roman Church-State to be an advocate of its own brand of faith-based fascism. *Ecclesiastical Megalomania* includes the complete text of the *Donation of Constantine* and Lorenzo Valla's exposé of the hoax.

*Education, Christianity, and the State*
J. Gresham Machen Trade paperback $9.95

Machen was one of the foremost educators, theologians, and defenders of Christianity in the twentieth century. The author of several scholarly books, Machen saw clearly that if Christianity is to survive and flourish, a system of Christian schools must be established. This collection of essays and speeches captures his thoughts on education over nearly three decades.

*Essays on Ethics and Politics*
Gordon H. Clark Trade paperback $10.95

Dr. Clark's essays, written over the course of five decades, are a major statement of Christian ethics.

*Gordon H. Clark: Personal Recollections*
John W. Robbins, editor Trade paperback $6.95

Friends of Dr. Clark have written their recollections of the man. Contributors include family members, colleagues, students, and friends such as Harold Lindsell, Carl Henry, Ronald Nash, and Anna Marie Hager.

*Historiography: Secular and Religious*
Gordon H. Clark Trade paperback $13.95

In this masterful work, Dr. Clark applies his philosophy to the writing of history, examining all the major schools of historiography.

*An Introduction to Christian Philosophy*
Gordon H. Clark Trade paperback $8.95

In 1966 Dr. Clark delivered three lectures on philosophy at Wheaton College. In these lectures he criticizes secular philosophy and launches a philosophical revolution in the name of Christ.

*Language and Theology*
Gordon H. Clark Trade paperback $9.95

There are two main currents in twentieth-century philosophy – language philosophy and existentialism. Both are hostile to Christianity. Dr. Clark disposes of language philosophy in this brilliant critique of Bertrand Russell, Ludwig Wittgenstein, Rudolf Carnap, A. J. Ayer, Langdon Gilkey, and many others.

*Logic* — Hardback $16.95
Gordon H. Clark — Trade paperback $10.95

Written as a textbook for Christian schools, *Logic* is another unique book from Dr. Clark's pen. His presentation of the laws of thought, which must be followed if Scripture is to be understood correctly, and which are found in Scripture itself, is both clear and thorough. *Logic* is an indispensable book for the thinking Christian.

*Lord God of Truth, Concerning the Teacher*
Gordon H. Clark and
Aurelius Augustine — Trade paperback $7.95

This essay by Dr. Clark summarizes many of the most telling arguments against empiricism and defends the Biblical teaching that we know God and truth immediately. The dialogue by Augustine is a refutation of empirical language philosophy.

*The Philosophy of Science and Belief in God*
Gordon H. Clark — Trade paperback $8.95

In opposing the contemporary idolatry of science, Dr. Clark analyzes three major aspects of science: the problem of motion, Newtonian science, and modern theories of physics. His conclusion is that science, while it may be useful, is always false; and he demonstrates its falsity in numerous ways. Since science is always false, it can offer no alternative to the Bible and Christianity.

*Religion, Reason and Revelation*
Gordon H. Clark — Trade paperback $10.95

One of Dr. Clark's apologetical masterpieces, *Religion, Reason and Revelation* has been praised for the clarity of its thought and language. It includes these chapters: Is Christianity a Religion? Faith and Reason; Inspiration and Language; Revelation and Morality; and God and Evil. It is must reading for all serious Christians.

*The Scripturalism of Gordon H. Clark*
W. Gary Crampton — Trade paperback $9.95

Dr. Crampton has written an introduction to the philosophy of Gordon H. Clark that is helpful to both beginners and advanced students of theology. This book includes a bibliography of Dr. Clark's works.

*Thales to Dewey:*
*A History of Philosophy* — Hardback $29.95
Gordon H. Clark — Trade paperback $21.95

This is the best one-volume history of philosophy in print.

*Three Types of Religious Philosophy*
Gordon H. Clark — Trade paperback $6.95

In this book on apologetics, Dr. Clark examines empiricism, rationalism, dogmatism, and contemporary irrationalism, which does not rise to the level of philosophy. He offers an answer to the question, "How can Christianity be defended before the world?"

*William James and John Dewey*
Gordon H. Clark — Trade paperback $8.95

William James and John Dewey are two of the most influential philosophers America has produced. Their philosophies of instrumentalism and pragmatism are hostile to Christianity, and Dr. Clark demolishes their arguments.

*Without A Prayer: Ayn Rand and the Close of Her System*
John W. Robbins — Hardback $27.95

Ayn Rand has been a best-selling author since 1957. *Without A Prayer* discusses Objectivism's epistemology, theology, ethics, and politics in detail. Appendices include analyses of books by Leonard Peikoff and David Kelley, as well as several essays on Christianity and philosophy.

## Theology

*Against the Churches: The Trinity Review 1989-1998*
John W. Robbins, editor — Oversize hardback $39.95

This is the second volume of essays from *The Trinity Review*, covering its second ten years, 1989-1998. This volume, like the first, is fully indexed and is very useful in research and in the classroom. Authors include: Gordon Clark, John Robbins, Charles Hodge, J. C. Ryle, Horatius Bonar, and Robert L. Dabney.

*Against the World: The Trinity Review 1978-1988*
John W. Robbins, editor — Oversize hardback $34.95

This is a clothbound collection of the essays published in *The Trinity Review* from 1978 to 1988, 70 in all. It is a valuable source of information and arguments explaining and defending Christianity.

*The Atonement*
Gordon H. Clark Trade paperback $8.95

In *The Atonement*, Dr. Clark discusses the covenants, the virgin birth and incarnation, federal headship and representation, the relationship between God's sovereignty and justice, and much more. He analyzes traditional views of the atonement and criticizes them in the light of Scripture alone.

*The Biblical Doctrine of Man*
Gordon H. Clark Trade paperback $6.95

Is man soul and body or soul, spirit, and body? What is the image of God? Is Adam's sin imputed to his children? Is evolution true? Are men totally depraved? What is the heart? These are some of the questions discussed and answered from Scripture in this book.

*By Scripture Alone*
W. Gary Crampton Trade paperback $12.95

This is a clear and thorough explanation of the Scriptural doctrine of Scripture and a refutation of the recent Romanist attack on Scripture as the Word of God.

*The Changing of the Guard*
Mark W. Karlberg Trade paperback $3.95

This essay is a critical discussion of Westminster Seminary's anti-Reformational and un-Biblical teaching on the doctrine of justification. Dr. Karlberg exposes the doctrine of justification by faith and works – not *sola fide* – taught at Westminster Seminary for the past 25 years, by Professors Norman Shepherd, Richard Gaffin, John Frame, and others.

*The Church Effeminate*
John W. Robbins, editor Hardback $29.95

This is a collection of 39 essays by the best theologians of the church on the doctrine of the church: Martin Luther, John Calvin, Benjamin Warfield, Gordon Clark, J.C. Ryle, and many more. The essays cover the structure, function, and purpose of the church.

*The Clark-Van Til Controversy*
Herman Hoeksema Trade paperback $7.95

This collection of essays by the founder of the Protestant Reformed Churches – essays written at the time of the Clark-Van Til controversy in the 1940s – is one of the best commentaries on those events in print.

*A Companion to The Current Justification Controversy*
John W. Robbins Trade paperback $7.95

This book includes documentary source material not available in *The Current Justification Controversy*, and an essay tracing the origins and continuation of this controversy throughout American Presbyterian churches.

*Cornelius Van Til: The Man and The Myth*
John W. Robbins Trade paperback $2.45

The actual teachings of this eminent Philadelphia theologian have been obscured by the myths that surround him. This book penetrates those myths and criticizes Van Til's surprisingly unorthodox views of God and the Bible.

*The Current Justification Controversy*
O. Palmer Robertson Trade paperback $9.95

From 1975 to 1982 a controversy over justification raged within Westminster Theological Seminary and the Philadelphia Presbytery of the Orthodox Presbyterian Church. As a member of the faculties of both Westminster and Covenant Seminaries during this period, O. Palmer Robertson was an important participant in this controversy. This is his account of the controversy, vital background for understanding the defection from the Gospel that is now widespread in Presbyterian churches.

*The Everlasting Righteousness*
Horatius Bonar Trade paperback $8.95

Originally published in 1874, the language of Bonar's masterpiece on justification by faith alone has been updated and Americanized for easy reading and clear understanding. This is one of the best books ever written on justification.

*Faith and Saving Faith*
Gordon H. Clark Trade paperback $6.95

The views of the Roman Catholic Church, John Calvin, Thomas Manton, John Owen, Charles Hodge, and B. B. Warfield are discussed in this book. Is the object of faith a person or a proposition? Is faith more than belief? Is belief thinking with assent, as Augustine said? In a world chaotic with differing views of faith, Dr. Clark clearly explains the Biblical view of faith and saving faith.

*God and Evil: The Problem Solved*
Gordon H. Clark Trade paperback $4.95

This volume is Chapter 5 of *Religion, Reason and Revelation,* in which Dr. Clark presents his solution to the problem of evil.

*God-Breathed: The Divine Inspiration of the Bible*
Louis Gaussen Trade paperback $16.95

Gaussen, a nineteenth-century Swiss Reformed pastor, comments on hundreds of passages in which the Bible claims to be the Word of God. This is a massive defense of the doctrine of the plenary and verbal inspiration of Scripture.

*God's Hammer: The Bible and Its Critics*
Gordon H. Clark Trade paperback $10.95

The starting point of Christianity, the doctrine on which all other doctrines depend, is "The Bible alone, and the Bible in its entirety, is the Word of God written, and, therefore, inerrant in the autographs." Over the centuries the opponents of Christianity, with Satanic shrewdness, have concentrated their attacks on the truthfulness and completeness of the Bible. In the twentieth century the attack was not so much in the fields of history and archaeology as in philosophy. Dr. Clark's brilliant defense of the complete truthfulness of the Bible is captured in this collection of eleven major essays.

*The Holy Spirit*
Gordon H. Clark Trade paperback $8.95

This discussion of the third person of the Trinity is both concise and exact. Dr. Clark includes chapters on the work of the Spirit, sanctification, and Pentecostalism. This book is part of his multi-volume systematic theology that began appearing in print in 1985.

*The Incarnation*
Gordon H. Clark Trade paperback $8.95

Who is Christ? The attack on the doctrine of the Incarnation in the nineteenth and twentieth centuries was vigorous, but the orthodox response was lame. Dr. Clark reconstructs the doctrine of the Incarnation, building and improving upon the Chalcedonian definition.

*The Johannine Logos*
Gordon H. Clark Trade paperback $5.95

Dr. Clark analyzes the relationship between Christ, who is the truth, and the Bible. He explains why John used the same word to refer to both Christ and his teaching. Chapters deal with the Prologue to John's Gospel; *Logos* and *Rheemata;* Truth; and Saving Faith.

*Justification by Faith Alone*
Charles Hodge Trade paperback $10.95

Charles Hodge of Princeton Seminary was the best American theologian of the nineteenth century. Here, for the first time, are his two major essays on justification in one volume. This book is essential in defending the faith.

*Karl Barth's Theological Method*
Gordon H. Clark Trade paperback $18.95

*Karl Barth's Theological Method* is perhaps the best critique of the Neo-orthodox theologian Karl Barth ever written. Dr. Clark discusses Barth's view of revelation, language, and Scripture, focusing on his method of writing theology, rather than presenting a comprehensive analysis of the details of Barth's theology.

*Logical Criticisms of Textual Criticism*
Gordon H. Clark Trade paperback $3.25

Dr. Clark's acute mind enables him to demonstrate the inconsistencies, assumptions, and flights of fancy that characterize the science of New Testament criticism.

*New Testament Greek for Beginners*
J. Gresham Machen Hardback $13.95

Long a standard text, *New Testament Greek for Beginners* is extremely helpful in the study of the New Testament in the original Greek. It may profitably be used by high school, college, and seminary students, either in a classroom setting or in self-study. Machen was Professor of New Testament Literature and Exegesis at Princeton Theological Seminary and the founder of Westminster Theological Seminary and the Orthodox Presbyterian Church.

*Predestination*
Gordon H. Clark Trade paperback $10.95

Dr. Clark thoroughly discusses one of the most controversial and pervasive doctrines of the Bible: that God is, quite literally, Almighty. Free will, the origin of evil, God's omniscience, creation, and the new birth are all presented within a Scriptural framework. The objections of those who do not believe in Almighty God are considered and refuted. This edition also contains the text of the booklet, *Predestination in the Old Testament.*

*Sanctification*
Gordon H. Clark Trade paperback $8.95

In this book, which is part of Dr. Clark's multi-volume systematic theology, he discusses historical theories of sanctification, the sacraments, and the Biblical doctrine of sanctification.

*Study Guide to the Westminster Confession*
W. Gary Crampton Oversize paperback $10.95

This *Study Guide* may be used by individuals or classes. It contains a paragraph-by-paragraph summary of the *Westminster Confession,* and questions for the student to answer. Space for answers is provided. The *Guide* will be most beneficial when used in conjunction with Dr. Clark's *What Do Presbyterians Believe?*

*A Theology of the Holy Spirit*
Frederick Dale Bruner Trade paperback, $16.95

First published in 1970, this book has been hailed by reviewers as "thorough," "fair," "comprehensive," "devastating," "the most significant book on the Holy Spirit," and "scholarly." Gordon Clark described this book in his own book *The Holy Spirit* as "a masterly and exceedingly well researched exposition of Pentecostalism. The documentation is superb, as is also his penetrating analysis of their non-scriptural and sometimes contradictory conclusions." Unfortunately, the book is marred by the author's sacramentarianism.

*The Trinity*
Gordon H. Clark — Trade paperback $8.95

Apart from the doctrine of Scripture, no teaching of the Bible is more fundamental than the doctrine of God. Dr. Clark's defense of the orthodox doctrine of the Trinity is a principal portion of his systematic theology. There are chapters on the Deity of Christ; Augustine; the Incomprehensibility of God; Bavinck and Van Til; and the Holy Spirit; among others.

*What Calvin Says*
W. Gary Crampton — Trade paperback $10.95

This is a clear, readable, and thorough introduction to the theology of John Calvin.

*What Do Presbyterians Believe?*
Gordon H. Clark — Trade paperback $10.95

This classic is the best commentary on the *Westminster Confession of Faith* ever written.

## Clark's Commentaries on the New Testament

| | | |
|---|---|---|
| *Colossians* | Trade paperback | $6.95 |
| *Ephesians* | Trade paperback | $8.95 |
| *First Corinthians* | Trade paperback | $10.95 |
| *First John* | Trade paperback | $10.95 |
| *First and Second Thessalonians* | Trade paperback | $5.95 |
| *New Heavens, New Earth* (*First* and *Second Peter*) | Trade paperback | $10.95 |
| *The Pastoral Epistles* | Hardback | $29.95 |
| (*1* and *2 Timothy* and *Titus*) | Trade paperback | $14.95 |
| *Philippians* | Trade paperback | $9.95 |

All of Clark's commentaries are expository, not technical, and are written for the Christian layman. His purpose is to explain the text clearly and accurately so that the Word of God will be thoroughly known by every Christian.

## The Trinity Library

We will send you one copy of each of the 59 books listed above for $500 (retail value $800), postpaid to any address in the U.S. You may also order the books you want individually on the order form on the next page. Because some of the books are in short supply, we must reserve the right to substitute others of equal or greater value in The Trinity Library. This special offer expires October 31, 2006.

# Order Form

NAME ________________________________________

ADDRESS ________________________________________

________________________________________

TELEPHONE ________________________________________

E-MAIL ________________________________________

Please:

❑ add my name to the mailing list for *The Trinity Review.* I understand that there is no charge for single copies of *The Review* sent to a U. S. address.

❑ accept my tax deductible contribution of $ ________ .

❑ send me ____ copies of *The Current Justification Controversy.* I enclose as payment U.S. $ _________.

❑ send me the Trinity Library of 59 books. I enclose U.S. $500 as full payment.

❑ send me the following books. I enclose full payment in the amount of U.S. $ _________ for them.

________________________________________

________________________________________

________________________________________

________________________________________

The Trinity Foundation
Post Office Box 68
Unicoi, Tennessee 37692
Website: http://www.trinityfoundation.org/
United States of America

Shipping: Please add $5.00 for the first book, and 50 cents for each additional book. For foreign orders, please add $6.00 for the first book and $1.00 for each additional book.